SCANDAL PROOF

Do Ethics Laws Make Government Ethical?

G. Calvin Mackenzie

with Michael Hafken

BROOKINGS INSTITUTION PRESS
Washington, D.C.

Library of Congress Cataloging-in-Publication data

Mackenzie, G. Calvin.
    Scandal proof : do ethics laws make government ethical? / G. Calvin
Mackenzie with Michael Hafken.
        p.   cm.
Includes bibliographical references and index.
    ISBN 0-8157-5402-7 (cloth : alk. paper)—ISBN 0-8157-5403-5 (pbk. :
alk. paper)
        1. Political ethics—United States.   2. Civil service ethics—United
States.   3. Conflict of interests—United States.   4. Executive
departments—United States.   I. Title: Do ethics laws make government
ethical?.   II. Hafken, Michael.   III. Title.
    JK468.E7 M33 2002   2002009135
    172'.2'0973—dc21   CIP

9 8 7 6 5 4 3 2 1

The paper used in this publication meets minimum requirements of the
American National Standard for Information Sciences—Permanence of Paper
for Printed Library Materials: ANSI Z39.48-1992.

Typeset in Minion

Composition by R. Lynn Rivenbark
Macon, Georgia

Printed by R. R. Donnelley and Sons
Harrisonburg, Virginia

FOR PETER B. WEBSTER
the most ethical man I know

Contents

Preface

America now has an ethics policy. It is comprehensive and it has profound effects. This book is an analysis—a policy analysis, to use the conventional term—of America's efforts to regulate the ethical behavior of federal employees. The focus is primarily on executive branch employees, particularly those in high-ranking positions. Equally important questions have emerged about judicial and congressional ethics, some of which have been wisely explored elsewhere, but they are not the subject of this book.[1]

This effort will look at the broad movement to elevate and fortify the integrity of executive branch employees through the imposition of a steadily broadening set of constraints on who may become a federal employee, how one may behave in office, and what one may do after departing from federal service. The analysis poses these central questions:

—How did the current framework of ethics regulation evolve?

—What have been the primary objectives of the ethics reform movement?

—Have those objectives been accomplished?

—What has all this effort cost?

—Do the benefits justify the costs?

—Where should ethics reform go from here?

Chapter 1 offers an introduction to the subject matter. Chapter 2 reviews the history of corruption in national politics and the emergence of legislative and administrative efforts to protect government integrity. The focus is narrowed in chapter 3 to the period that begins with President John F.

Kennedy's executive order in 1961 that established a new framework for ethics regulation and follows the momentum initiated by that action up to the present time. Close attention is paid to the arguments and political pressures that drove the expansion of ethics regulation, and especially to the motives and goals of the reformers.

Chapter 4 considers the products of this forty-year evolution: the current fabric of ethics regulation and the network of federal agencies and offices that have been established to define and enforce the new rules. What are the rules now? How are those rules enforced and by whom? How is the work environment in the federal government different today? How has the process of entering government changed, especially at the highest levels?

The impact of ethics regulation is the subject of chapter 5. Based upon several sources of newly gathered empirical evidence, an assessment is made of whether federal government integrity is different today from what it was before 1961. The effects of the regulations imposed since 1961 are compared with the aims of those who initiated or supported them. Have their objectives been accomplished?

Chapter 6 explores the costs of ethics regulation, both the formal dollar costs of managing a very expansive program of integrity protection and the less formal and less easily discernible costs of requiring tens of thousands of federal employees to file detailed reports on their personal finances and adjust their behavior in and after government service to a growing set of ever-more confining constraints on their behavior.

Finally, chapter 7 seeks to answer the following questions: How much improvement in the integrity of public officials has the ethics regulation effort accomplished? What have been the costs? Do the benefits justify the costs? What lessons have been learned from the experience of the decades that followed 1961? Where should reform efforts go from here to ensure the integrity of the federal government?

Discussions of integrity in government, such as this one, are often fogged in clouds of passion. No one is neutral on this topic. Many Americans think their government is corrupt and that corruption is endemic. Some think the corruption stems from the American system of campaign finance and the symbiotic relationships between special interests and government employees. Others think even worse—that public officials are on the take or have gone into government service only to get something for themselves. A national poll conducted by the Presidential Appointee Initiative in the summer of 2001, for example, found that nearly nine in ten Americans believed that presidential appointees were driven by personal ambition in accepting administration jobs. And a third of the respondents thought that appointees were less honest than most Americans.[2]

But some public employees and their defenders feel equally strongly that public servants have been badly and unfairly maligned. Among the millions of people who work for the federal government, they argue, the vast majority are loyal, hard-working, and dedicated to the highest standards of integrity and fair play. The few who violate these norms, they further argue, unfairly taint the reputations and performance of all public servants.

No one should set sail on this raging sea expecting a smooth ride. And Michael Hafken and I do not. We offer some assessments that are outside the mainstream of opinion about government integrity. And we offer suggestions for reform that challenge the conventional wisdom. We expect some controversy and criticism will follow from the analysis we offer and from the conclusions we draw from it.

We welcome that. We believe that government has a profound responsibility to act with integrity and that public servants should be held to high standards of accountability for their performance. But we also believe that government should be a hospitable and supportive environment for the most creative and most talented people. Any effort to enhance the integrity of government must be mindful of its broader impacts and costs.

We hope this book stirs the pot of public debate and inspires some reflection on what has been done over the past four decades to make public servants more honest. We believe that the efforts to improve the integrity of government have suffered from a dearth of such debate and an even greater shortage of careful analysis of their impacts. If we succeed at all in stimulating more analysis, more debate, more careful weighing of the costs and benefits of ethics regulation, then our own objectives in writing this book will be fully met.

The research, ideas, and insights of many people contributed to this analysis of federal ethics regulation. How does one acknowledge adequately the intellectual debts accumulated over thirty years?

I first encountered issues of government ethics as a graduate student preparing a doctoral dissertation on the presidential appointments process. I have continued to study and write about that process ever since, interviewing hundreds of helpful and candid government officials. In addition, I have worked for a congressional commission that studied the ethics of members of Congress, I have been an ethics trainer for a large federal agency, and I had the honor to serve as a member and chair of the Commission on Governmental Ethics and Election Practices in my home state of

Maine. In each of those roles, I have been educated and enriched by people who honestly, and sometimes painfully, discussed with me their personal experiences with the modern ethics regime. While I cannot acknowledge them all individually, I hope all of them who read this book will be aware of the debt I owe them.

Two among those, however, deserve special mention. J. Jackson Walter, the first director of the Office of Government Ethics, was my initial and best tutor on all aspects of federal ethics regulation. I have benefited from Jack's insights over the past two decades almost as much as I have enjoyed his friendship.

The other is Peter B. Webster. No person I have encountered in my professional life better embodies the traits of probity, fairness, compassion, and courtesy that ought to be the model for all public servants. I am grateful for Peter's friendship over many years, but thankful as well for the opportunity I had to serve the people of Maine as his colleague and in the bright light of his constant and shining example.

During the preparation of the manuscript, I worked closely with several people whose contributions were indispensable. Larry Benenson was a tireless contributor during the summer he spent as an intern at the Brookings Institution. Katie Barnes and Jeff Brink at Colby College helped answer many of the last-minute research questions that bedevil any author. At the Presidential Appointee Initiative (PAI), I had the daily blessing of the hard work and imaginative contributions of Anna Gallagher, Judith Labiner, Sherra Merchant, Erin Murphy, and Gina Russo. Carole Plowfield and Sandra Stencel, my wonderful partners at PAI, read the entire manuscript with great care and offered suggestions that improved it significantly.

My friends at the Brookings Institution Press, Robert Faherty, Lawrence Converse, Susan Woollen, Janet Walker, and Rebecca Clark, managed the production and marketing of this book with good cheer and remarkable skill and efficiency. Specifically, Colleen McGuiness edited the manuscript, Inge Lockwood proofread the pages, and Robert Elwood provided an index. It has been a pleasure to work with them again.

The three reviews of the manuscript commissioned by the press provided a wealth of constructive comment and insight. To Frank Anechiarico, Jim Pfiffner, and Susan Tolchin, and to all others who offered commentary on this book, I express my deep gratitude and full release from responsibility for any errors it might yet contain.

At every step of the way, indeed in all of the projects we have undertaken together over the past two decades, it has been a constant delight to work with Paul C. Light. I am grateful to him for his friendship and good humor, for his brilliant understanding of governance in America, and for his tireless efforts to distribute my work through his own.

The greatest debt I owe here is the one reflected by the name on the book's cover. From the day we conceived this book until the day it went to press, Michael Hafken was my intellectual comrade-in-arms. A tireless and highly skilled researcher, Michael spent hours collecting forms, talking with officials in government agencies, compiling intricate spreadsheets, and undertaking so many of the other, often tedious tasks that transform ideas into research and then into deductions and conclusions. Day after day, I walked into his office and said something like, "Michael, I wonder if we could find out who actually looks at all these forms or how many newspaper stories there were on that subject." I always knew how many days of hard work it would take to track down the answers. But I also always knew that Michael would find a way to get it done and to accomplish the task with all of the attention to detail that excellent research requires. That he always did so with such good humor—at least when I was around—only added to my deep respect for him.

G. CALVIN MACKENZIE

Men constantly try to escape
From the darkness outside and within
By dreaming of systems so perfect that
no one will need to be good

T. S. ELIOT
"Choruses from 'The Rock'"

Introduction

For young William O. Douglas, who later served for more than three decades on the U.S. Supreme Court, the call changed his life. It came from his friend Joseph P. Kennedy, who had left his post at the Securities and Exchange Commission (SEC) in September 1935. "When there was a vacancy on the commission later that year, Joe Kennedy told me he wanted to get 'the Boss' to name me to the office. So he took me over to see FDR, who greeted me warmly and said, 'You're my man.' I was confirmed on January 23, 1936."[1]

It is hard to imagine an agency more fraught with temptation for those who had larceny in their hearts than the Securities and Exchange Commission. What brilliant investment decisions one could make knowing what one learns at the SEC. But no investigation of Douglas's ethics was held before he took this job. No background investigation. No grueling interviews in the White House. No intrusive questionnaires and lengthy forms to complete. No vetting. No financial disclosure. No duplicative Senate investigations. It was enough that the president wanted him and the Senate approved him. That exercise of collective political judgment, following the Constitution, was the only vetting that William O. Douglas—or any other public official of the time—was required to endure.

The appointment process had been that way since the beginning of the Republic and would stay that way for another generation. For most political nominees, getting into government was simple and quick. Serving in government may have required a financial sacrifice, but it was a minor inconvenience to most of those whose primary career was in the private sector. Barriers to entry were low; discomforts of service were few. Public officials routinely maintained other jobs and professions during their government service. Many made daily decisions that affected corporations and other enterprises in which they had a personal financial interest. In the two world wars, the country turned to its most experienced business leaders to manage key elements of the mobilization effort. They retained status and salary in the corporations they headed and became government advisers known as "dollar-a-year men."

Where private and public interests clashed, there was widespread faith that the latter would prevail. It was a faith based on an optimistic view of human nature and a confidence that the political leaders who chose and approved administrators and judges would make honesty a key criterion of what Alexander Hamilton had called "fitness" for public service. As Hamilton wrote:

> To what purpose then require the co-operation of the Senate [in approving nominations]? I answer, that the necessity of their concurrence would have a powerful, though, in general, a silent operation. It would be an excellent check upon a spirit of favoritism in the President, and would tend greatly to prevent the appointment of unfit characters from State prejudice, from family connection, from personal attachment, or from a view to popularity. In addition to this, it would be an efficacious source of stability in the administration.
>
> . . . A man disposed to view human nature as it is, without either flattering its virtues or exaggerating its vices, will see sufficient ground of confidence in the probity of the Senate, to rest satisfied, not only that it will be impracticable to the Executive to corrupt or seduce a majority of its members, but that the necessity of its co-operation, in the business of appointments, will be a considerable and salutary restraint upon the conduct of that magistrate.[2]

Hamilton's faith was sometimes tested. Some widely accepted practices in earlier times would not pass muster today. For example, public officials were paid retainers by corporations, and public officials were provided generous gifts and services from those whose interests they regulated. And sometimes the faith that the public interest would prevail was seriously abused by government employees who knowingly violated their public trust for personal enrichment.

But the country prospered and grew, the American people came to rely more on their national government for programs and protections, and the occasional scandal did little to thwart a pattern of broad public trust in government. Even during the Gilded Age in the second half of the nineteenth century, when large economic interests shamelessly promoted their own purposes through largesse to government officials and when many cities and some states were run by party machines fueled by what one of their bosses called "honest graft," efforts at reform found only sporadic and shallow support from most Americans. For much of American history, though it was a common topic of conversation and the stimulus for an occasional muckraking wingding, corruption in government was not a matter that kept many Americans awake at night.

No surprise that. Until after World War II, most Americans found that their lives intersected rarely and only marginally with government. The national government provided few goods or services to its people and imposed no taxes on all but a handful of them. In 1939 less than 3 percent of the American people paid any income taxes. The federal budget on the eve of World War II was less than $10 billion, and the government in Washington, D.C., performed few of the functions that today consume more than a fifth of the American gross domestic product. If some government officials occasionally trespassed the boundaries of propriety, it was a matter of some entertainment but little consequence to most Americans whose lives were no more affected by corruption in Washington than in Bolivia or Bombay.

However, the ethics of public officials were not unregulated. The historical pattern of reform has been for occasional, highly visible public scandals to yield calls for regulation, which often resulted in new laws or rules. A post office scandal during Andrew Jackson's presidency inspired Postmaster General Amos Kendall to produce the first code of ethics for any government agency in 1829. When government officials were caught accepting money to lobby for the fraudulent claims of some veterans after the Mexican-American War, Congress in 1853 enacted legislation to prohibit the practice. After revelations of significant profiteering during the Civil War, a new statute prohibited federal officials from accepting compensation in exchange for aid to private citizens in matters in which the United States was a party.

The Progressive Era also yielded some new ethics regulations, most in response to corruption that took place during World War I. A law signed in 1917 prohibited any supplementation of the salaries of federal employees. In 1919 Congress banned War Department procurement officials from engaging in any private business dealings with the federal government for two years after leaving federal service.

But nothing in U.S. history matched the impetus for change that emerged in the middle decades of the twentieth century. Government was growing; the New Deal and especially the Second World War were powerful stimuli to that growth. The national government took on social welfare functions that had never before been public responsibilities. And the Second World War and the cold war that followed brought permanent changes to America's self-perception and to its role in the world. Big government arrived in mid-century, and it never left.

And as government grew, the American people came to be stakeholders as they had never been before. The federal government began to provide pensions for the elderly. It started to provide health care insurance for the poor and the aged. It began to subsidize local education, to build a grid of federal highways, and to shoot rockets into space. It constructed a vast network of support for its military veterans and a safety net for its disadvantaged citizens. And it became the greatest military power the world had ever known, with attendant peacekeeping responsibilities around the globe.

As the federal government took on all these new roles, its tentacles reached more deeply into American life, especially American economic life. More and more corporations, and more and more citizens, came to depend on government contracting decisions for their livelihood. A relatively small government expenditure—a few hundred million dollars, for example—could mean life or death for a company that received or failed to receive the contract that directed that expenditure.

As the stakes grew, the stakeholders and the stake-seekers got better organized. They mastered the intricacies of the appropriations and procurement processes. They learned who the key decisionmakers were, and they sought out ever more ingenious ways of communicating with them and influencing their decisions: advertising, campaign contributions, lobbying, and so on.

Most of these activities were entirely legal. A few were not. When the line was crossed, the federal government often responded by drawing the line more clearly and by imposing new laws and rules to fortify it. "There ought to be a law," the critics would declare. And, invariably, a new law soon appeared.

Those efforts accumulated and grew into the most elaborate system of ethics regulation ever devised by any national government. Some of the foundation of that system came into place early in U.S. history, but most of the edifice has been constructed in the past forty years.

These changes have occurred without much broad scrutiny or assessment. Potential critics found difficulty sailing into the prevailing wind of Washington opinion that anything that promised "more ethics" was undoubtedly good and anyone who opposed new ethics regulations was undoubtedly standing in the way of "more ethics." Ethics regulation has been the motherhood issue of recent times—too politically costly to oppose even when the direct benefits were uncertain or broader consequences troublesome.

The modern momentum for ethics regulation began in 1961 when a distinguished committee of legal scholars called for a review of all ethics laws. Its great landmark, the Ethics in Government Act of 1978, was constructed nearly a quarter century ago. In all of that time, the steady tightening of restrictions on the behavior of federal employees has been the subject of too little study and too little balanced evaluation. The time for a comprehensive assessment is long overdue.

CHAPTER TWO

The Way
We Were

Logically, an analysis such as this would begin by characterizing the context of recent developments. What was the past like, and how is the present different? But when the topic is government ethics, the past is difficult to characterize, at least accurately and empirically. There are tales to tell—plenty of them. Political scandals are part of the warp and woof of American public life.

But are they the norm or are they aberrations? Here the going is much tougher. Beyond the anecdotes, very little evidence survives from history that would help answer the question: On the whole, has the government in Washington, D.C., been honest or not? Were graft and corruption endemic or exceptional? We simply cannot be certain.

These are hard political substances to measure in the best of circumstances. What is corruption? What is public integrity? What is too much of the former or enough of the latter? Is government more honest this year than it was last? Even if anyone had sought to develop and maintain an annual integrity index for government, the problems in doing so might have been overwhelming. But no record exists of anyone making the effort, and so we have little more than anecdotes and the passing judgments of historians and political scientists to help us determine what the old days were like and whether government in times past was more or less honest on the whole than it is now.

Frank Anechiarico and James B. Jacobs note in their study of corruption in New York that calculating whether official corruption has increased over time is difficult for several reasons.

First, corrupt transactions, such as bribery, are rarely reported to the authorities or survey researchers. Second, there are no statistics on the number of corrupt acts committed by public officials or the percentage of transactions or decisions tainted by official corruption. Third, the definition of corruption has changed over time to include more types of official and private conduct. Because a corruption rate has never been calculated or even estimated, it is impossible to determine whether particular anticorruption campaigns and controls reduce corruption.[1]

An added problem is that of changing standards and then of changing laws. Some practices, once very common, would now get the practitioners indicted in federal courts. What was once defined as acceptable gift giving is now defined as bribery. Public officials once held additional jobs outside government, which now is a criminal offense. "Dollar-a-year men" organized much of the mobilization for World War I; conflict-of-interest regulations now prohibit the practice. As Suzanne Garment noted in her study of contemporary political scandals:

> A good deal of our current scandal activity stems from heightened ethical sensitivities and a distaste for what were once accepted practices in American politics. For instance, today's political campaigns may not seem ethically attractive to the modern eye, but fund-raising methods now are far more honest than in the days when cash changed hands under the table and individuals did their buying of congressmen in secret. In the same way, when we look down the list of recent political scandals that have embroiled executive branch officials, we quickly see that many of them involved offenses that would never have become known at any other time in our political history or would not have been considered worthy of serious, sustained attention.[2]

There also is the problem of multiple windows. When one window closes on proscribed transactions, another may open. The apparent success of an organization in reducing one form of behavior may simply be the failure to recognize that similar transactions now occur at another window. At one time, for example, an agent seeking to influence a government decision on a contract might have offered a kickback to the public employee responsible for the contract decision. Today, confronted with more and better-enforced antibribery regulations, the agent will devote his attention to legal campaign contributions as a way to influence government decisions. The old form of corruption may be diminished, but the new form flourishes. One window closes, another opens.

Finally, there is the problem of magnitudes. The population is bigger, government employment is larger, the federal budget has multiplied, federal contracts are more plentiful, and so on. All the ingredients of corruption—more people with more to gain from government activity—have expanded. So even if instances of corruption are more plentiful now than in the past, can we still properly conclude that government and government officials are more corrupt? As a portion of all government actions and decisions, those tinged with corruption, though larger in number, may be much smaller in percentage.

All of these considerations impose heavy caveats and burdens of proof on analysts who seek to assess the state of public integrity in Washington and to assess the steps the federal government has taken to regulate the behavior of its own employees. No one can tread confidently on this very soft ground.

Pictures from the Past

Looking back over the years before 1961 reveals a long line of government leaders and government employees who were honest and honorable, who were diligent in seeking to define the public interest and to make policies that served that definition. But exceptions to that pattern are evident at every stage in our history. The self-interests, and sometimes even the unchecked greed, of public officials periodically corrupted the governing process.

For a substantial portion of U.S. history, government functioned as a vast employment agency for the partisans whose candidate became president. A political system fueled by the desire of its most active participants to get jobs for themselves and their friends would encourage some rule-bending. A careful reading of that portion of American history yields some surprise that corruption was not greater even than it was. In fact, the spoils system fell into the discipline of its own patterns and routines, and these helped to keep its corrupting tendencies at bay. A recent analysis by Robert Maranto found that turnover under the spoils system was far from what legend suggests.

> In the party change from John Quincy Adams, [Andrew] Jackson dismissed only about 10% of federal personnel. Low-level workers were

seldom removed, and experienced clerks, auditors, and employees with needed technical skills (as in assay office and patent office) were nearly always retained. Dismissals were particularly unusual in field offices, but even in Washington, about two thirds of the federal officials serving in 1828 were still on the rolls in 1831. Many of the absent one third had left voluntarily, died, or been dismissed for poor work or moral failings rather than their politics. Others were dismissed because Jackson allowed his appointees to pick their own teams to facilitate management efficiency.

Later presidents were less principled. Still, in the mid-1800s, fewer than one third of federal offices were redistributed after a party change in the White House.[3]

The character of the government in Washington for the first half century of the American experience was shaped significantly by its small size and limited agenda. On the fortieth anniversary of George Washington's inauguration in 1829, for example, there were only 625 federal employees in Washington, only 318 of them in the executive branch.[4]

But the role of the government had begun to change with the Louisiana Purchase in 1803. This addition of vast new lands led to demands on Congress to appropriate funds for what we now call infrastructure and economic development: canals, dredging, bridges, and so on. Millions of acres of land also were available to distribute to citizens. Land speculators, traders, and others who wished to get rich in these new lands soon realized the benefit of having friends in Washington who could help them get the appropriations or the land rights they needed. Claims agents soon emerged as a growing force in the nation's capital, and in those days of largely undefined and unregulated ethical obligations, government officials themselves sometimes took on clients whom they aided in making claims on the government.

The brief Mexican War of 1846–48 added to the new practice of citizens employing government officials to help them get money or benefits from the government. Under the laws of the time, Congress was required to appropriate funds to pay any valid claim filed by a citizen showing that federal troops had destroyed private property. A claimant had no more effective way to get such an appropriation than to secure the representation of a member of Congress or other well-placed government official. And acting as agents for these claims was a useful way for government employees to supplement their incomes. But the practice soon grew out of control, and in 1853 Congress passed a law prohibiting all federal employees from representing any private client in a claim before the government.[5] This was the first example in what would later become a host of laws enacted to define the boundaries of ethical behavior for federal employees.

When the government in Washington undertook to provide arms and materiel for the Union forces in the Civil War, this unprecedented government activity yielded unprecedented government corruption. Never before had the federal government spent so much money or undertaken so sweeping an enterprise. If its administrative systems and its administrative talent often may not have been up to the task, its ethical standards clearly were not. The enterprises of fielding, equipping, and supplying the Union forces were littered with payoffs and kickbacks and rip-offs. Middlemen bribed public officials to get contracts for their clients, vessels chartered by the government never left port, and goods delivered under government contract often fell far short of the negotiated standards. A House investigating committee could only conclude that "such gross and unblushing frauds would have cost those who participated in them their heads under any system than our own."[6]

In 1864, faced with ample evidence of federal employees receiving compensation for helping private businesses secure government contracts, Congress enacted new legislation prohibiting all officers and employees of the federal government, members of Congress included, from receiving any compensation for services they might provide to any private citizen in any matter pending before the government.

The end of the Civil War released a powerful and pent-up new energy in America. The industrial revolution was in full flower. Railroad tracks zippered communities together across every state and territory, and in 1869 they linked the Atlantic and Pacific. A national market opened up and fed the country's ravenous, acquisitive appetites. In politics, patronage was king, and government service seemed but one more avenue to the cornucopia of opportunities that filled the era. Historian Vernon Louis Parrington compared the "come and get it" morality of the time to a "Great Barbeque." "To a frontier people," he wrote, "what was more democratic than a Barbeque, and to a paternalistic age what was more fitting than that the state should provide the beeves for roasting. Let all come and help themselves. As a result the feast was Gargantuan in its rough plenty."[7]

The election of Ulysses S. Grant in 1868 and the subsequent appointment by Grant of many aides and officials too little constrained by principle and too heavily devoted to self-interest opened the door to some dark moments in the history of public administration in America. "Friends, family, and officials of the Grant administration embodied this corpulent spirit conspicuously, attracting charges of financial and political corruption," writes archivist Timothy Rives.[8]

One scandal followed another during Grant's presidency, and while the president himself seemed incorruptible, his unyielding loyalty to friends and allies who were abundantly corruptible kept his administration constantly on the defensive. The most notable of the Grant scandals was the Whiskey Ring, evidence of which began to emerge in the early 1870s.

This was a fairly simple scheme to defraud the Treasury of tax money that should have been paid by the distillers of whiskey, principally in Missouri. But it was done on a massive scale and eventually corrupted Treasury and revenue officials in Missouri and Washington and involved Grant's trusted assistant and private secretary, Gen. Orville E. Babcock. It was a very lucrative venture. From November 1871 to November 1872, the Whiskey Ring leaders and the four involved distilleries each received between $45,000 and $60,000—money that should have been collected by the U.S. Treasury.[9] The magnitude of the scandal, not its ingenuity, was perhaps its most notable characteristic. By the time the court cases had run their course, 238 men had been indicted, and almost half of them were ultimately convicted.[10]

Like other scandals of the Grant administration and of the second half of the nineteenth century, the key elements were growing and very profitable industries, a desire to avoid government regulation or taxation, and a patronage or "spoils" system that seemed unduly hospitable to government employees more interested in personal gain than public service.

Massive national parties had become the dominant political model in mid-nineteenth-century America, fueled by the influx of immigrants and dominated by wily political bosses. The model of gentrified public service that emerged in the early decades under the Constitution of 1787 did not survive the election of Andrew Jackson in 1828. The brutal politics that preceded the Civil War and the vengeful politics that followed it held little appeal for the elites who had governed America in its early decades. More practical men took over.

And they brought with them a new set of attitudes, a common view of politics as a set of exchange relationships in which those who gave got. Those who loyally gave their votes got food and fuel and housing. Those who worked for the party or the boss got jobs in government. The harder they worked, the better the jobs. Those in government who delivered favorable programs and policies to burgeoning economic interests got rewards of a different sort: cash retainers, generous gifts, lucrative jobs, and assistance for family and friends.

Like American society and the American economy, concepts of honor and duty, indeed all of what might be conceived as public morality, were in transition during and after the Civil War. "It could be found in state and municipal governments, in business and finance and transportation, and even in the professions," wrote historians Samuel Eliot Morison and Henry Steele Commager. "There was almost everywhere a breakdown of old moral standards, and to many it seemed that integrity had departed from public life."[11]

No one captured the spirit of the age more pungently than George Washington Plunkitt, a state senator and one of the "bosses" of New York's Tammany Hall political organization, reflecting on politics at the end of the nineteenth century:

> Everyone's talking these days about Tammany men growin' rich on graft, but nobody thinks of drawing the distinction between honest graft and dishonest graft. There's all the difference in the world between the two. Yes, many of our men have grown rich in politics. I have myself. I've made a fortune out of the game, and I'm gettin' richer every day, but I've not gone in for dishonest graft—blackmailing gamblers, saloon keepers, disorderly people, etc. and neither has any of the men who have made big fortunes in politics.
>
> There's an "honest" graft, and I'm an example of how it works. I might sum up the whole thing by sayin' "I seen my opportunities, and I took 'em."
>
> Just let me explain by examples. My party's in power in the city, and it's going to undertake a lot of public improvements. Well, I'm tipped off, say, that they're going to lay out a new park in a certain place. I see my opportunity, and I take it. I go to that place, and I buy up all the land that I can in that neighborhood. Then the Board of This or That makes the plans public, and there is a rush to get my land, which nobody cared particularly for before.
>
> Ain't it perfectly honest to charge a good price and make a profit on my investment and forethought? Of course it is. Well, that's honest graft.[12]

The mindset of a government employee whose job was only secure until the next election was very different from that of a gentleman performing a public service or a civil servant in government for the long haul. Uncertain what the future might hold, the spoilsmen had incentives to take more from their time in government than just the honor of service and a small government salary. And when a new and very powerful political actor—the corporation, or the trust as it was then widely known—appeared on the Washington scene in the second half of the nineteenth century, temptations began to materialize that even an honest spoilsman found hard to resist.

The Gilded Age brought massive concentrations of capital that had no precedent in American public life. And the new corporations often found that they needed government. They needed government to subsidize their growth with favorable tax policies, to protect them from the evils of competition, and to supply them with land and with rights to exploit resources. Many of these corporations understood the rules of the time: To get something, you must give something. Many corporations spent their money aggressively to buy influence with government decisionmakers, sometimes to buy those decisionmakers. And government became a subject of manipulation in ways it never had been before, manipulation that often simply overwhelmed government's capacity to protect its own integrity.

The famous Crédit Mobilier scandal of 1872 is an apt example of the way some corporations got what they wanted from government. The Union Pacific Railway Company set out to bribe members of Congress to get their help. Union Pacific established a front corporation, Crédit Mobilier of America, to construct a railroad. Crédit Mobilier sought land grants and direct subsidies from Congress to encourage railroad construction, often telling Congress that construction costs were much higher than in fact they were. To encourage congressional support, stock in Crédit Mobilier was given to many influential Washington politicians, including important Republicans in Congress and Vice President Schuyler Colfax. Congress was generous in its response. The railroad was built, and the so-called investors in Crédit Mobilier (including the gifted members of Congress) enjoyed the benefits.[13]

Scandals occurred with such frequency and with such publicity after the Civil War that the public soon seemed inured to them. Many Americans came to view them as simply business as usual. The taint of scandal rarely ended a political career. James A. Garfield, for example, one of the members of Congress found to hold Crédit Mobilier stock, became president less than a decade later. As journalism became national, leading practitioners such as Joseph Pulitzer found that the scandals provided a steady stream of good copy. And muckraking reporters had much fodder for their investigative skills. But efforts to protect the integrity of government and the public serv-ice were slow in coming.

By the late 1870s, however, the laws of political physics began to apply and the new force of corporate influence produced an opposite, if not equal, counterforce—a reform movement. The reformers worried about many things, but the increasingly odiferous image of government and political leaders corrupted by the influence of money was their prime target. To many of them the first line of defense was to take the power to staff the gov-ernment, or at least much of it, away from the people who won the elec-tions. And the instrument for that, a civil service, became the prime objec-tive of the anticorruption forces.

The first civil service bill was introduced in Congress in 1865. In 1871 Congress authorized President Grant to set up a civil service commission to write rules for hiring and promotion in government. Grant did so with minimal enthusiasm, and the Republican Congress soon stopped appropri-ating funds even for this limited incursion into new territory.[14]

When civil service did come, with the Pendleton Act of 1883, it covered only about 12 percent of federal employees, but the camel's nose was under the tent and the battle for honest government was at full tilt. A new class of reformers was emerging around the country, largely middle class and urban. Its members wanted changes in the rules of elections and nominations, greater separation of administration from politics, and a more scientific approach to government. Many reformers also wanted government to begin to exercise some control over the economic forces that seemed then to dom-inate American society.

This was not an idle fear. Government in the second half of the nine-teenth century was still a small enterprise, with about twenty thousand employees in Washington and barely twice that many in all of the armed services. The great corporate trusts employed many more people than that and seemed able to run roughshod over the public interest whenever it con-flicted with their own.

But what good would it do to empower government to regulate business if the people doing the regulating were appointed by easily corrupted politi-cians or were themselves easily bought by the interests they were supposed to regulate? So the reform agenda was crowded with ideas designed to free government decisionmaking from the tight grip of the large economic interests and the often complicit bosses of the political parties. And between 1883 and the First World War, as the data in table 2-1 indicate, the success

Table 2-1. *Legislative Successes of the Government Reform Movement, 1883–1920*

Year	Legislation	Purpose
1883	Pendleton Act	Created a federal civil service
1887	Interstate Commerce Act	Created the first independent regulatory commission, the Interstate Commerce Commission
1889	State actions	Established use of the Australian, or secret, ballot
1903	State actions	Initiated use of direct primaries for party nominations of candidates
1908	State actions	Established the initiative, referendum, and recall to give citizens direct access to the ballot and a way to remove elected officials
1913	Sixteenth Amendment	Authorized Congress to impose and collect a federal income tax
1913	Seventeenth Amendment	Popular election of U.S. senators
1920	Nineteenth Amendment	Female suffrage

of that agenda began to roll back the interests of the large corporations and create a different standard of public integrity.

The First World War marked the end of the Progressives as a significant force in American politics. Attention turned to getting American troops into battle and ensuring they had the arms and supplies they needed. The government again found that it had to reach out for the administrative talent necessary to manage this effort, and it turned to the private sector. Many business executives came to work on the war effort, not as government employees but on loan from their corporations. And while the practice appears in retrospect to have provided the management skills critically needed by a government at war, it was widely criticized at the time by labor leaders and other reformers. To them, borrowing talent from the private sector opened the floodgates to special interests that would use their access to direct the flow of government contracts and to make construction and production decisions that favored the companies whose executives, albeit on loan to the government, were at the table.

The appetite for war profits and the corrupt tendencies they set in motion forced Congress to reconsider the use of the dollar-a-year men. Some employees of the Interior Department whose salaries were entirely subsidized by large charitable foundations initially stimulated congressional concern. In 1917 Congress enacted a governmentwide policy prohibiting any federal employee from accepting salary from a nongovernment source.[15] This came to be known as the supplementation of salary ban, and it remains in effect to this day. Its purpose was to ensure that federal employees were not biased or otherwise unduly influenced in their decisions by their nongovernment sponsors.

The First World War also created opportunities for federal employees to profit from their access to secret government information. A company seeking contracts with the War Department, for example, would be willing to pay handsomely for information about the department's plans for new weapons. When such employees left government service, they sometimes entered the waiting arms of War Department suppliers who wanted the inside information they brought with them. Recognizing that this created unfair advantages for certain companies and undue pressure on government employees, Congress prohibited former federal employees from representing outside interests before their former agencies for two years after they left government service. But this ban was limited only to those who had served in the executive branch during the war.

After the war, according to historians, America returned to normalcy. And the nation was soon engulfed in one of history's most notable political scandals. The Progressive movement had faded from political importance by this time, leaving as its final legacy the Eighteenth Amendment and the prohibition of alcohol. One of the consequences of Prohibition was massive lawbreaking in every segment of society as Americans continued to consume what was now a banned substance. In boardrooms, in country clubs, in neighborhood speakeasies, and even in the White House, the alcohol continued to flow.

The passing of the Progressive era also restored business to its earlier place among society's saints and refueled what the journalist William Allen White had called the "alliance between government and business for the benefit of business."[16] The election of 1920 brought a president who mirrored almost perfectly the corrupt tendencies of the time. Warren G. Harding had few noticeable political principles, but he possessed a rock-solid faith in free enterprise. The dominant economic interests could not have had a better friend in the White House.

Harding appointed underqualified cronies to his cabinet and to many other high-ranking positions in government. He and they mixed freely with lobbyists for large corporations. When the secretary of the interior, Harding's old friend Albert B. Fall, came to the White House and asked Harding to issue an executive order transferring control of three major oil reserves in the West from the Navy to the Interior Department, Harding did so without hesitation. Fall then began to grant favorable leasing rights to his friends in the oil industry.

But this was no simple act of friendship. In exchange for his help, oil executives, especially Harry F. Sinclair of the Sinclair Consolidated Oil Company, lined the pockets of Albert B. Fall. For his help in providing leases in one of the three reserves—in Teapot Dome, Wyoming—Fall received Liberty Bonds from Sinclair worth almost $400,000.[17] Eventually, congressional investigations and court cases uncovered the facts and both Fall and Sinclair spent time in jail. While the most memorable, Teapot Dome was only one of several major scandals that bubbled up from the moral swamp of the Harding years.

Nevertheless, government misbehavior during the Harding era prompted little legislative response. Laws against bribery were already on the books, and they provided ample opportunity for prosecutors to punish the crooks from both the public and private sector.

When the New Deal emerged a few years later, government began to spread its tentacles into vast jurisdictions where it had rarely or never gone before. The Great Depression of the 1930s had taken the bloom off the business rose, and Franklin D. Roosevelt's administration, with ample public support, began to construct a broad edifice of business regulation. At the same time, government spending on new social welfare and economic recovery programs grew rapidly. When the country entered the Second World War, federal expenditures quickly escalated to unprecedented levels, and once again the country turned to experienced business leaders to manage the war effort. As before, many of these leaders retained their ties to their corporate employers and continued to receive compensation from those employers while they worked as dollar-a-year men or without-compensation advisers in government.

Sensitivity to the conflict-of-interest potential inherent in these arrangements had grown since the First World War, and the War Production Board began to conduct background checks of those who came to work for government while retaining ties to former employers. Care was also taken to assign these on-loan executives to positions in which they would not be involved in decisions that affected the interests of their corporate patrons.[18]

As government grew during the 1930s and 1940s, the task of monitoring government ethics grew more complicated. More government employees were engaged in a far broader range of activities that intersected much more often with powerful economic interests than ever before. Those who worried about the opportunities for corruption inherent in these changes began to focus their efforts not so much on the personal behavior of individual government employees as on the regularity and consistency of government procedures. In 1939 Congress enacted the Administrative Reorganization Act, which created the Executive Office of the President, expanded presidential staffing, and increased the ability of the president to exercise firmer controls over the growing number of government agencies and employees. In 1946 the Administrative Procedures Act established a legal framework to guide the regulatory and rule-making activities of all federal agencies. Ensuring openness and fairness were important goals of this act.

When World War II ended, the federal government did not shrink to its prewar dimensions. Most of the New Deal functions, if not the agencies that first managed them, remained intact. A Defense Department was created to oversee the large standing armed forces that were kept on duty after the war. Big government was here to stay.

A larger government needed more senior managers, and the number of those who came through the presidential appointment process grew steadily in the postwar years. The federal government took on an expansive array of tasks and turned routinely to these in-and-outers to manage them. They were often people who left the private sector for a relatively short term of public service and found themselves unfamiliar or ill at ease with the public work environment. For some, the consequences were ethically toxic, with significant reverberations for the presidents who brought them into government.

The Truman administration, especially in its second term, was dogged by scandals involving both career employees and political appointees. A broad pattern of influence peddling was uncovered at the Reconstruction Finance Corporation, and the Internal Revenue Service experienced the worst scandal in its history. In 1951 Democrats in Congress, motivated in no small part by embarrassment at the misdeeds that had occurred at a time when their party was in the majority, undertook detailed investigations of ethical violations in the executive branch.

The most important of these was conducted by Paul Douglas, a first-term Democratic senator from Illinois. The Douglas investigation identified the growth of the federal government as a major contributor to changes in the ethical environment and indicated a range of inappropriate activities for which federal employees should be punished or dismissed.[19]

With a storm brewing in the press and Congress, President Harry S. Truman tried to compete for moral leadership by sending his own message to Congress on ethical standards for public employees. A remarkably radical document for the time, it recommended a number of ethical strictures on public officials, including the requirement that presidential appointees, members of Congress, and some other federal officials make full public disclosure of their personal finances.

> Public office is a privilege, not a right, and people who accept the privilege of holding office in the Government must of necessity accept that their entire conduct should be open to inspection by the people they are serving. With all the questions that are being raised today about the probity and honesty of public officials, I think all of us should be prepared to place the facts about our income on the public record. We should be willing to do this in the public interest, if the requirement is applied equally and fairly to the officials of all three branches of our Government.[20]

Unwilling to let Truman get credit for improving ethics in government, Republicans in Congress prevented the enactment of legislation that might have resulted from the combined impact of the Truman message and the Douglas hearings.

The 1952 campaign brought a Republican assault on "the mess in Washington" played to the tune of "Korea, Communism, and Corruption." Shortly after his inauguration, President Dwight D. Eisenhower ordered the institution of security checks—Federal Bureau of Investigation (FBI) full-field investigations—on all of his senior appointees. But the Eisenhower victory only led to a new wave of scandal and public dismay. While most of the misdeeds were minor notes on the ethical scale, the melody was unending, reaching a crescendo with the 1958 resignation under fire of Sherman Adams, Eisenhower's chief of staff and the second most powerful man in the administration. Adams had accepted expensive personal gifts from individuals who were under regulatory investigation. Like its predecessor, the Eisenhower administration came to an end under an ethical cloud.

New Directions

Had this book been written on the eve of the Kennedy administration, what might it have concluded? America has had a steadily growing and increasingly more sophisticated government. Government had much more to do in 1960 than ever before, and a large number of public servants with a broad range of skills and talents were needed to conduct the public's business. Furthermore, the history of federal administration was pockmarked with scandals petty and large. No meaningful way existed to count or measure these scandals, or to draw up a balance sheet of government integrity. While the vast majority of public employees seemed to perform their duties honestly, every era had exceptions, and sometimes those exceptions were highly visible and deeply corrosive of public faith in government.

In addition, few legislative initiatives had been undertaken to curb the potential for corruption in public employees. Beyond some fundamental laws against bribery, self-dealing, representing individuals in claims against the government, and supplementation of salary, the legal code was largely silent about the ethical obligations of federal employees. Their backgrounds were not subject to anything more than superficial scrutiny when they entered government, they could invest their money as they pleased, their personal finances were private matters, and no limits were set on what they could do after they left government service.

In the view of most political leaders of the time, the solutions to the problem of ethics in government were already in place. First, the key to government integrity was the existence of effective mechanisms of political accountability. These included a free and competitive press, open and contested elections, and other devices such as citizen-initiated recalls of public officials. Second, government officials were insulated from the bias of external influences on their decisions by supplementation of salary prohibitions and civil service rules. Third, as an ultimate protection, proscribed behavior was defined in statutes and violations were prosecuted in court.

The dominant notion prevailed that the day-to-day business of government would be handled by career civil servants, freed from external political pressures and encased in a culture of professional devotion to the public interest, and that leadership would fall to a small group of talented and loyal people chosen by the president. Accountability would be imposed on the president and his appointees by the quadrennial electoral judgments of the people, by the occasional exception taken by the Senate to the confirmation of an appointee who seemed not to meet acceptable standards of competence or integrity, and by the courts when necessary. Little effort was made to define ethical standards in language and rules or to shape prophylactic strategies to head off ethical problems.

All that began to change in 1961. The focus of ethics regulation began to shift to individual federal employees and to new approaches that assumed all federal employees were vulnerable to corruption and that their personal lives would have to be regulated and their personal privacy sacrificed to better protect the public interest. This approach started slowly and evolved gradually, but by the end of the twentieth century an entirely new culture of ethics regulation had taken firm root in Washington and was spreading its boughs through every aspect of the government's business and across the path of every senior federal employee, career and noncareer alike.

CHAPTER THREE

Building the
Bastion,
1961–2000

More than a century of episodic, situational responses to unique ethics controversies had produced by 1960 an accumulation of laws that were inconsistent, overlapping, and, in some cases, contradictory. A private initiative, a study of the entire fabric of federal ethics regulation by the Association of the Bar of the City of New York, called attention to the problem and identified the need for a comprehensive federal review of ethics laws.

Shortly after entering office, President John F. Kennedy appointed a three-member Advisory Panel on Ethics and Conflict of Interest in Government to study the problems raised by this study.[1] The committee delivered its report in March 1961. It concluded, as one of its authors later summarized, that the federal laws governing conflicts of interest were "archaic, inconsistent, overlapping, ineffective to achieve their purposes, and obstructive to the government's efforts to recruit able personnel."[2]

A few weeks later President Kennedy sent a message to Congress, calling for new legislation to recodify the conflict-of-interest and other ethics statutes and to modify some of them to fit contemporary realities, especially with respect to the employment of part-time and short-term government consultants. "No responsibility of government is more fundamental," Kennedy declared in his message to Congress, "than the responsibility of maintaining the highest standards of ethical behavior by those who conduct the public business. There can be no dissent from the principle that all officials must act with unwavering integrity, absolute impartiality and complete devotion to the public interest."[3]

The Kennedy initiative represented the beginning of a movement toward a new kind of ethics protection: reliance on rules and stringent enforcement of those rules. The appeal of this approach was compelling, as Robert N. Roberts and Marion T. Doss Jr. note:

> Rule-driven ethics had a number of advantages over character-focused ethics. Rules could be written down and explained. Ambiguity was eliminated. Investigatory and adjudicatory procedures could be used to resolve disputes over compliance.[4]

The Kennedy approach was the first of many steps over the next four decades that created the system of contemporary ethics regulation. While one law—the Ethics in Government Act of 1978—is the centerpiece of that system, the construction process has rarely stopped. Building the bastion against corruption has been the work of every administration and nearly every Congress. In understanding this construction process, it is essential to view it in the same frame with the political dynamics that drove it.

Laying the Foundation

Like all public policies, ethics policies have been shaped by politics. They are the cumulative responses to decades of political positioning and calculations of political opportunity and advantage. Those officials who participated in the construction of ethics policies always did so with a sharp eye on their public appearance—often more than on their practical impacts. That was true in 1961, and it has been true ever since.

President Kennedy's initiative was not apparently driven by any scandals or fear of future scandals in his administration. He noted in his message to Congress that "venal conduct by public officials in this country has been comparatively rare—and the few instances of official impropriety that have been uncovered have usually not suggested any widespread departure from high standards of ethics and moral conduct."[5] He seems to have been following the momentum of the previous two years in which the Eisenhower administration suffered several embarrassing incidents of personal misconduct and several congressional committees began to explore the broad legal issues of regulating public integrity.[6] The report of the Association of the Bar of the City of New York added to this momentum.

Congress responded to President Kennedy's message with the enactment of P.L. 87-849 in October of 1962. The new legislation took effect the following January and had two major objectives. One was to clean up the inconsistencies and overlaps in the existing body of ethics legislation by recodifying it. The second was to make government service easier for those who were not full-time, long-term government employees. Nothing in the legislation, however, added any significant legal constraints to those that were already in effect at the outset of the Kennedy administration.

Kennedy also acted on his own during this period, issuing an executive order and sending memoranda to department heads on ethics matters. Executive Order 10939, signed on May 5, 1961, prohibited federal employees from engaging in outside employment inconsistent with their public duties, from receiving nongovernment compensation for any activity (for example, lectures, articles, public appearances) that fell within the normal scope of their duties, and from accepting gifts when they had reason to believe that the donor's interests might be affected by the actions of the employee's agency.

Lyndon B. Johnson took even broader action in the first year of his presidency. Shortly after becoming president, he asked his staff to review the ethical standards for government employees. He sought, noted John W. Macy Jr., his chief personnel adviser, to set the right "ethical tone" for his administration.[7] This effort resulted in the issuance of Executive Order 11222 on May 8, 1965.

Like Kennedy earlier, Johnson noted that,

> although the overwhelming majority of federal employees experience absolutely no problem in this regard, there are some whose duties on occasion place them in difficult or awkward situations. . . . The special problems faced by federal employees lie in the area of judgment, propriety, and good taste. Obviously these cannot be legislated or prescribed by Order or regulation.[8]

Yet Johnson's order took ethics regulation further than it had ever gone before. Much of the executive order was a restatement or redefinition of earlier proscriptions and caveats. But Johnson stipulated not simply that federal employees avoid carefully defined conflicts of interest and abuses of office but also that they avoid the appearance of those. The appearance standard is in Part 3(c) of Section 201 of the order and states:

> (c) It is the intent of this section that employees avoid any action, whether or not specifically prohibited by subsection (a), which might result in, or create the appearance of—

(1) using public office for private gain;

(2) giving preferential treatment to any organization or person;

(3) impeding government efficiency or economy;

(4) losing complete independence or impartiality of action;

(5) making a government decision outside official channels; or

(6) affecting adversely the confidence of the public in the integrity of the Government.

The appearance standard has been part of the fabric of ethics regulations since its inclusion in Johnson's executive order. But it has always been a frustration to those seeking to comply with it and those charged with enforcing it.

Executive Order 11222 added another new dimension to ethics regulation: the requirement that federal employees report the details of their personal finances. Part IV of the order mandated that presidential appointees make full disclosure of their personal finances within thirty days of assuming office and update those statements periodically thereafter. It also directed the Civil Service Commission to work with agency heads to develop financial reporting procedures for other federal employees. In all cases, the financial reports would be confidential and subject to review by the Civil Service Commission or the appropriate agency head, but not available to the public.

The inconsistencies that followed in the implementation of this requirement led to some backlash in the ranks. "The extension of it to large numbers of employees by agency action contributed to the cries of 'invasion of privacy,'" wrote Macy, the Civil Service Commission chair at the time. "It was apparent that some agency managers were overly zealous, or misinterpreted the requirement, or opposed it and extended its coverage beyond the point of necessity."[9]

The purpose of the confidential reporting requirement was to help federal employees avoid conflicts of interest by having them go through the periodic discipline of reviewing their own financial assets and obligations, then submitting them to a counselor at the Civil Service Commission or in their agency who would review the reports and discuss with the employees any potential conflicts of interest. As Macy noted, "the mere process of preparing a declaration of holdings brought the attention of the employee to the possible relationship of his personal holdings to the obligations of his public responsibility."[10]

The Kennedy and Johnson years were largely unmarked by political scandal or evidence of ethical impropriety. Kennedy succeeded in encouraging

Congress to repair the inconsistencies in federal ethics law, and both presidents issued executive orders that were primarily hortatory in articulating ethical standards for federal employees. Johnson broadened those standards to include appearances as well as actual violations, and he ordered the one significant enlargement of the existing scheme of ethics regulation with the requirement in 1965 that federal officials make confidential disclosure of their personal finances.

In neither case were the new policies direct responses to specific problems, and they did not result from any careful analysis of policy options that might realistically raise the level of public integrity in government. They were driven instead largely by the desire to persuade the public of each president's commitment to high ethical standards. That the actions taken may have had little impact on ethical behavior was of less concern than the political importance of affecting that appearance.

The Johnson administration made one other, indirect and unintended, contribution to the evolution of ethics regulation. As the Vietnam War dragged on, public dissatisfaction with it grew. And as evidence accumulated that the president's optimistic statements about Vietnam did not comport with the reality of the fighting there, what came to be known as a credibility gap began to corrode the relationship between the American people and the government in Washington, D.C. Public trust in government to "do the right thing" began to decline.[11]

That steady decline in public trust worried public officials and soon put them on the hunt for some visible response. Reaction to the presidency of Richard M. Nixon accelerated all of this, turning the hunt to a passion, a passion that led to the most comprehensive regulation ever of the behavior of public employees.

Watergate and Its Aftermath

In the most famous speech of his political life, delivered to a national audience as his place on the 1952 Republican ticket was in grave jeopardy, Richard Nixon said, "I have a theory, too, that the best and only answer to a smear or an honest misunderstanding of the facts is to tell the truth. . . . A man that's to be President of the United States . . . must have the confidence of all the people."[12] No small irony, then, that Nixon did more than any other figure in the twentieth century to diminish confidence in government.

The Watergate scandal is a pivotal event in American political history in many ways. It led, at a minimum, to a substantial restructuring of campaign finance rules. It generated political momentum for the War Powers Act, the Congressional Budget and Impoundment Control Act, more diligent congressional oversight of intelligence activities, more aggressive exercise of the Senate confirmation power, limits on the use of executive agreements, and many other alterations in the balance between executive and legislative power. Watergate inspired Congress to expand its own institutional capacities and to complete one of the most sweeping rearrangements of power in its history. And it caused Congress to retrieve from obscurity and revitalize the constitutional impeachment power that it had not applied to a president in more than a century. Like a powerful tornado, Watergate changed everything in its path.

But nowhere were the changes more profound than in the rules and procedures that regulate the ethical behavior of public officials. The momentum was relentless as president and Congress made new laws and issued new orders intended to build permanent fortifications against every form of perfidy ever known to government. "Ethics" became the rallying cry of the time, and "Pour it on!" the standard cheer. In committee rooms, on the floor of Congress, in executive orders, and presidential speeches, politicians of both parties and every ideology competed to be the most passionate and eloquent advocate of government integrity. They imposed restrictions on each other and on themselves, arguing that the public interest could be served only by encasing public servants in a thick armor of protection against their own venal instincts.

There must be no more Watergates, they all agreed. And most were certain that the best insurance was an increasingly detailed set of "Thou shalt not's" (many with criminal penalties for violators) and an elaborate network of procedures designed to deter even the most remote threat to the public trust.

Watergate was not a single misdeed, not even a single set of misdeeds. It is a term now applied to a broad range of misbehavior committed over several years in the 1970s by members of the Nixon administration and reelection staff. Some of those activities were illegal under existing laws, some were excesses of campaign fund-raising and campaign activities, some were expansions of executive authority beyond what was politically acceptable at the time, and some were merely bad form. Table 3-1 identifies the individuals whose alleged wrongdoing became part of the Watergate scandal and the sanctions they received, if any.

Much of the subsequent effort directed at ethics regulation was a response to Watergate, an attempt to ensure that such a large-scale government scandal

Table 3-1. *Crimes of the Watergate Scandal*

Name	Charge(s)	Outcome or disposition
Bernard L. Barker	1. Burglary, wiretapping, conspiracy 2. Conspiracy to violate Daniel Ellsberg's psychiatrist Lewis Fielding's rights	1. Pleaded guilty. Sentenced to eighteen months to six years in prison. 2. Pleaded not guilty. Convicted. Placed on three years probation.
Virgilio Gonzolez	Burglary, wiretapping, conspiracy	Pleaded guilty. Sentenced to one to four years in prison.
E. Howard Hunt Jr.	Burglary, wiretapping, conspiracy	Pleaded guilty. Sentenced to thirty months to eight years in prison and fined $10,000.
G. Gordon Liddy	1. Burglary, wiretapping, conspiracy 2. Conspiracy to violate Fielding's rights 3. Refusing to testify before a House committee	1. Pleaded not guilty. Convicted. Sentenced to six years and eight months to twenty years in prison. 2. Pleaded not guilty. Convicted. Sentenced to one to three years in prison. 3. Pleaded not guilty. Convicted. Sentenced to a suspended six-month prison term and placed on probation for one year.
Eugenio Martinez	1. Burglary, wiretapping, conspiracy 2. Violating Fielding's rights	1. Pleaded guilty. Sentenced to one to four years in prison. 2. Pleaded not guilty. Convicted. Placed on three years probation.
James W. McCord Jr.	Burglary, wiretapping, conspiracy	Pleaded not guilty. Convicted. Sentenced to one to five years in prison.
Frank A. Sturgis	Burglary, wiretapping, conspiracy	Pleaded guilty. Sentenced to one to four years in prison.
Charles W. Colson	Conspiracy, obstruction of justice, conspiracy to violate Fielding's rights	Pleaded not guilty to Fielding's charge. Pleaded guilty to charge of obstruction of justice. All other charges dropped. Sentenced to one to three years in prison and fined $5,000.

John W. Dean III	Conspiracy to obstruct justice and defraud the United States	Pleaded guilty. Sentenced to one to four years in prison.
John D. Ehrlichman	Conspiracy, obstruction of justice, making false statements to the FBI, making a false statement to a grand jury or court	Pleaded not guilty. FBI charge dropped; convicted on all other charges. Sentenced to serve thirty months to eight years in prison.
H. R. Haldeman	Conspiracy, obstruction of justice, perjury	Pleaded not guilty. Convicted. Sentenced to thirty months to eight years.
Frederick C. LaRue	Conspiracy to obstruct justice	Pleaded guilty. Sentenced to serve six months in prison.
Jeb Stuart Magruder	Conspiracy to obstruct justice and defraud the United States	Pleaded guilty. Sentenced to a prison term of ten months to four years.
Robert C. Mardian	Conspiracy to obstruct justice	Pleaded not guilty. Convicted. Sentenced to serve ten months to three years in prison.
John N. Mitchell	Conspiracy, obstruction of justice, perjury, making a false declaration to a grand jury or court, lying to FBI agent	Pleaded not guilty. FBI charge dropped. Convicted of all other charges. Sentenced to two and a half to eight years in prison.
Herbert L. Porter	Making false statements to FBI agents	Pleaded guilty. Sentenced to serve thirty days of a five- to fifteen-month sentence.
Dwight L. Chapin	Making false statements before a grand jury	Convicted on two out of four counts. Sentenced to ten to thirty months in prison.
Donald H. Segretti	Distributing illegal campaign literature	Pleaded guilty. Sentenced to six months in prison.
George A. Hearing	Fabricating and distributing illegal campaign literature	Pleaded guilty. Sentenced to one year in prison.
Egil Krogh Jr.	Violating Fielding's rights	Pleaded guilty. Sentenced to two to six years in prison.

(continued)

Table 3-1. *Crimes of the Watergate Scandal (Continued)*

Name	Charge(s)	Outcome or disposition
Richard G. Kleindienst	Refusing to testify fully to the Senate Judiciary Committee	Pleaded guilty. Sentenced to one month of unsupervised probabtion. Received suspended sentence of one month and fined $100.
Edward L. Morgan	Participating in a conspiracy to create fraudulent $576,000 income tax deduction for President Richard M. Nixon	Pleaded guilty. Sentenced to serve four months of a two-year sentence.
Robert L. Vesco	Conspiracy to obstruct justice, endeavoring to obstruct justice	Fled country and became fugitive in Costa Rica.
Jack L. Chestnut	Accepting an illegal $12,000 campaign contribution	Pleaded not guilty. Convicted. Sentenced to serve four months in prison and fined $5000.
Jake Jacobsen	Perjury before a grand jury, bribery	Perjury charge dropped on a technicality. Pleaded guilty to charge of bribery. Sentencing deferred.
Harold L. Nelson	Conspiracy	Pleaded guilty. Sentenced to serve four months in prison and fined $10,000.
Herbert Kalmbach	Violating the Federal Corrupt Practices Act, promising federal employment as a reward for political activity and for support of a candidate	Pleaded guilty. Sentenced six to eight months in prison and fined $1,000.
26 individuals[a]	Violating campaign finance laws	Pleaded guilty or convicted. Fined or sentenced to short jail sentence.

SOURCE: Congressional Quarterly, *Watergate: Chronology of a Crisis* (Washington, 1975); and Facts on File, *Facts on File: Weekly World News Digest with Cumulative Index* (New York, 1975).

a. David L. Parr , Stuart H. Russell, Norman Sherman, John Valentine, George Steinbrenner III, John H. Melcher Jr, Orin E. Atkins, Tim M. Babcock, Harding L. Lawrence, H. Everett Olson, Harry Dent, Ray Dubrowin, Jack A. Gleason, Russell DeYoung, Claude C. Wilde Jr., Charles N. Huseman, William Lyles Sr, Richard L. Allison, Francis X. Carroll, John L. Loeb, Harry Heltzer, James Allen, Thomas V. Jones, William W. Keeler, C. Arnholt Smith, Raymond Abendroth.

would not happen again, and an endeavor to restore the American people's trust in government after Watergate had diminished it. Yet few of the rules and procedures established after Watergate in the name of government ethics bore much relevance to the kinds of specific misdeeds that composed Watergate. And if the current scheme of ethics regulation had been in effect in 1972, it would have done little to detect or deter most of the behavior that contributed to the Watergate scandal. There was no absence of law during Watergate, only an absence of law-abiding.

A New Mentality

The Watergate affair made one powerful contribution to the explosion in new ethics policies that reverberated over the following several decades. It gave birth to a "post-Watergate mentality" that survived long after the scandal that inspired it. It survives to this day.

What are the elements of this mentality? First, public servants are suspect. Their good character cannot be assumed. We charge them with responsibility for managing large programs with enormous budgets and deep consequences. Such responsibilities are fraught with temptation for self-dealing. We must, therefore, build legal walls to protect the public interest from the self-interests of public servants. Because good character cannot be assumed, it cannot be trusted. Other means are necessary to ensure public integrity.

Second, protection against the most common forms of ethical indiscretion by public servants is not enough. Laws must protect against all possible breakdowns of public integrity. Rules must contemplate not best-case behavior or normal-case behavior but worst-case behavior. We must deny public servants not only the ability to represent clients in cases pending before the government but also the right to represent any private client in any matter. We must prohibit public employees from earning any income outside of their government salary, not just income from sources that pose a potential conflict of interest with their public duties. We must define as posing a potential conflict of interest all financial assets that fall into the penumbra of public responsibilities, not merely those of sufficient magnitude to lead a reasonable person into temptation. In the post-Watergate mentality, all rules quickly become worst-case rules.

Third, the only reliable protection against the corrupt instincts of public servants is the law. Instruction, encouragement, and guidance, though desirable, are not sufficient to ensure a satisfactory level of public integrity. Trust in the capacity of the political processes of election and appointment to produce honorable leaders and hold them accountable for their behavior is also insufficient. Only strict, detailed, and rigid laws—usually accompanied by criminal sanctions—can provide the protection the public needs from the venality of its own public servants.

Fourth, to effect this newly energized ethical regulation of public servants, a new corps of regulators must be engaged. They must be specialists in the ethics laws they implement, free of other distractions, and equipped with budgets and resources to write more elaborate new rules, to investigate any charge that the public trust has been violated, and to prosecute alleged violators to the full extent of the law. The post-Watergate mentality has put ethical sentries not only at the gates but also at nearly every door and window of the federal establishment.

The Post-Watergate Political Dynamic

The Watergate scandal was not the sole parent of the post-Watergate mentality. In a number of ways, the scandal only accelerated trends that were emergent before the Watergate burglars stumbled into the hands of the law on June 17, 1972. Washington in the 1970s had already begun to form some of the habits that Watergate only galvanized and helped to institutionalize.

Divided government was one of those. When the Democrats regained control of Congress from the Republicans in the 1954 congressional elections, six years of divided government—the White House in the hands of one party and Congress in the hands of the other—began. That was the longest period of divided government in U.S. history up to that point. But it seemed an aberration, attributable largely to President Eisenhower's personal popularity at a time when the Democrats were, by every measure, the dominant party. The restoration of Democratic hegemony for the eight years beginning in 1961 seemed only to verify the anomaly. But then came Richard Nixon, not only with the narrowest of victories in 1968, but the greatest of landslides in 1972. The rapid deterioration of the solid Democratic South in presidential elections indicated to many that divided government might be more common in the future than it had even been in the past. There was prescience in this view, for divided government occurred 64 percent of the time in the second half of the twentieth century compared with only 16 percent in the first half.

As Washington politicians acclimated to this new likelihood, they began to think of legislative-executive relations in different ways. Old concepts of majority and minority did not fit the new realities. And old practices of legislative-executive cooperation could no longer draw on the political energy that once sustained them. Institutional bickering came to replace partisan bickering, and Congress and the executive began to fortify themselves against each other. Nothing suffered more in this transition than mutual trust between the institutions. Constraints evaporated that once would have prevented Congress from defining detailed standards or imposing strict regulations on the president's appointees.

The skirmishes over ethics were part of a larger battle for control of the executive branch and its powerful capacity to influence public policy. As political scientists Gary W. Cox and Samuel Kernell have argued:

> Beyond presidential vetoes and the near-continuous tug of war over taxes and spending, divided government has also introduced another realm of competition between Congress and the presidency, which, though less public, is no less consequential for defining these institutions' respective roles in making public policy. We refer here to competition over control of the bureaucracy.
>
> . . . Under divided government, presidential efforts to administer the bureaucracy confront Congress's extensive prerogatives, thereby creating a battleground for political control.[13]

Many of the post-Watergate ethics regulations fell most heavily on business executives recruited or sought for appointments in Republican administrations. These were the men and women whose corporate experience prepared them for certain kinds of jobs in government, often dealing with the business sector from which they had come. And they were also the wealthiest of political appointees and therefore most likely to be affected by conflict-of-interest rules prohibiting certain kinds of financial holdings. But the congressional majorities of the time were increasingly liberal and often little sympathetic to the consequences of these rules for business executives.

When Ronald Reagan reached out to the business communities to recruit many of his appointees in 1981, he encountered unexpected reluctance to serve. "Legal and other regulatory constraints tend to bear more heavily on businessmen," said E. Pendleton James, Reagan's chief personnel recruiter. "The talent pool would be considerably enlarged if at least some of the major hurdles to public office could be removed or lowered."[14] But these recruiting difficulties caused few tears to be shed by the Democrats who controlled the Congresses that created many of the ethics regulations that so nettled the Reagan personnel recruiters.

Watergate also stimulated another trend that had preceded it, and that was the emergence of several powerful public interest groups in Washington. There had been public interest groups in the capital for many decades. They were often minor players in political debates, frequently dismissed by their detractors as "goo-goo's"; that is, good-government interests that could rarely match the political clout of much better financed special interests. But on the issue of government ethics, several of these public interest groups struck a rich vein of opportunity, functioning not simply as moral adjudicators but as moral entrepreneurs. For here was an issue on which the special interests had little to say. Who, after all, spoke for corruption or venality?

In the nineteenth century, when political parties depended on certain kinds of honest graft to dominate American politics, party leaders were able to direct most reform efforts into quiet oblivion. But in the 1970s, old-style honest graft was no longer in vogue, and political party leaders did not have much interest in discussions of public employee ethics. So, fueled by the constant pressure of public interest groups such as Common Cause, ethics became the motherhood issue of its time. Everyone was for ethics, the more the better.

And when the public interest groups suggested radical innovations to tighten the fabric of ethics regulation, few volunteers came forward to question their assumptions, challenge their suggestions, or demand proof of wrongdoing. This was one of those rare contemporary political imbalances when discouraging words were seldom heard. Father Robert Drinan, who as a member of Congress from Massachusetts in 1978 supported the Ethics in Government Act, later said, "Frankly, there was hysteria when this was going through. You wouldn't think of voting against the conflict of interest legislation, and you didn't examine it because who's going to really vote no anyway? . . . In those days after Watergate the assumption was sort of that everybody's a crook and we have to separate them out."[15]

No politician wanted to be on the side of less ethics. And those few who dared oppose the legislative proposals for more ethics laws usually did so on technical constitutional grounds or by suggesting that the consequences of these new laws might be worthy of more consideration than they were being given under the crushing wheels of the ethics bandwagon. There was little political comfort on the wrong side of this issue. And once Watergate took hold of the national consciousness, there was little doubt which was the wrong side—at least politically.

Finally, but equally important in the post-Watergate period, there was the force of momentum. Watergate did not begin the effort to raise levels of government employee integrity. That effort had been under way, however fitfully, for some time. Long-standing criminal statutes prohibited supplementation of salary and barred representation of private citizens in claims before the government. Some restrictions had been put in place decades earlier on the post-employment activities of certain government officials. Those and other ethics laws were recodified and upgraded in 1962. President Johnson in 1965 introduced the appearance standard and initiated confidential reporting of personal finances for federal officials.

Momentum was already under way when Watergate struck. So the post-Watergate mentality required escalations above and beyond previous efforts to define and enforce ethical standards. Private disclosure yielded to public disclosure. Ethics codes gave way to ethics laws. Restrictions on certain categories of federal employees were replaced by similar restrictions on all federal employees.

The response to Watergate was a powerful political force that built on all that came before Watergate. And what it ultimately produced was an array of ethics laws, rules, and procedures that had no precedent in the United States or in any other country in the history of the world. And no offspring of the post-Watergate mentality loomed larger than the Ethics in Government Act of 1978.

The Ethics in Government Act of 1978

When President Jimmy Carter signed P.L. 95-521 on October 26, 1978, he said that it was a response to "problems that developed in the highest levels of government in the 1970s."[16] The Ethics in Government Act pulled together several approaches to public integrity that had become popular in the aftermath of Watergate. The six principal theories underlying those details were as follows (see box 3-1).

1. Transparency is critical to deterrence. The more the public knows about its government leaders, especially about their financial interests, the less likely they are to use positions of authority to enrich themselves improperly.

2. Government leaders need careful definition and constant reminders of what constitutes a conflict of interest or abuse of office. Professional ethics counselors should review each official's financial holdings every year to detect and cure potential conflicts of interest.

Box 3-1. *Major Provisions of the Ethics in Government Act of 1978*

—Required annual public financial disclosure by the president, vice president, senior executive branch officials, members of Congress, and federal judges, and each filer's spouse and dependent children.

—Established the Office of Government Ethics to develop rules and regulations on ethical issues, conduct training programs, and monitor compliance with ethics requirements.

—Created restrictions on the post-government activities of federal employees.

—Established a mechanism for appointment of a special prosecutor to investigate and prosecute criminal allegations against the president, vice president, and cabinet officers.

---

3. All government officials, regardless of specific duties, should be subject to the same requirements of transparency and scrutiny.

4. The personal finances of immediate family members of government officials should be subject to much the same transparency and scrutiny as the officials' themselves.

5. When officials leave the government, rigid constraints should be placed on subsequent activities that might influence their former agency or government colleagues.

6. Permanent agencies should manage ethics regulation, and when charges are leveled at incumbent officials, special procedures must be followed because the normal enforcement authorities cannot be trusted to investigate impartially.

Making the Case

It took nearly a year and a half for the Ethics in Government Act to move through the legislative process, from introduction to law. During that time, the president and Congress engaged in extended debate that yielded insightful expressions of the motivations for new ethics regulation and, on the part of a few, a set of doubts and concerns about the utility and the costs of such regulation. The law has become the centerpiece of the contemporary scheme of ethics regulation; it is, therefore, worth exploring the hopes—and the fears—of the people who created it.

In the message to Congress that accompanied his ethics proposals, President Jimmy Carter indicated that he was following up on a campaign promise to assure the American people "that their government is devoted exclusively to the public interest" by establishing "far-reaching safeguards against conflicts of interest and abuse of the public trust by Government officials."[17]

Restoring the confidence of the American people in their government is a constant theme in the legislative history of the ethics act, a frequently cited justification for whatever sacrifices it imposes on those entering or remaining in public service. The Senate Governmental Affairs Committee said that the act would "preserve and promote the accountability and integrity of public officials and of the institutions of the Federal government" and that it would "increase public confidence in the government."[18]

During House debate, Rep. Tom Corcoran (R-Ill.) declared his support for the bill because "too many people believe that politicians are scoundrels seeking their own personal interest at the expense of the public interest. Each new national opinion survey conveys this growing lack of confidence in government. To reverse this growing cynicism, we need this landmark legislation before us today."[19] Rep. Richardson Preyer (D-N.C.) joined the call for passage to "help restore public confidence in government."[20] Rep. Lawrence Coughlin (R-Pa.) cited the necessity of counteracting the disillusion of the American people that resulted from "the continuing accounts of scandal." "The conflicts of interest, the misuse of public moneys, and the allegations of personal enrichment while in government service," he argued, "undermine the public faith."[21]

This theme was equally prominent on the Senate floor. Sen. Charles H. Percy (R-Ill.) called the legislation "a way to restore the basis for confidence in public officials and in the federal government."[22] Sen. Hubert H. Humphrey (D-Minn.) called the act a "major step toward a stronger, more accountable government which can better command and justify public confidence."[23]

Another steady refrain in the legislative history is the declaration that the ethics act achieves a proper balance between the rights of the public and the rights of federal employees. After detailing some of the extensive financial disclosure requirements in his proposal, President Carter said,

> The vast majority of government officials, of course, have always followed strict ethical standards. I respect their efforts and integrity, and I have carefully considered the new obligations that this legislation will place on them. The provisions of the act would strike a careful balance between the rights of these individuals to their privacy and

the right of the American people to know that their public officials are free from conflicts of interest.[24]

In its report on the bill, the House Post Office and Civil Service Committee declared that it was "providing a workable financial reporting and disclosure system for the executive branch which carefully balances the oftentimes competing interests of the public and the employees."[25]

Proponents of the legislation in both houses argued that the need for transparency trumped any claim to privacy. By entering public service, the dominant argument suggested, Americans surrender the right to privacy that is widely protected for private citizens.

What was the rationale for the loss of privacy this legislation imposed on federal employees? The Senate Governmental Affairs Committee offered a five-part answer:

1. Public financial disclosure will increase public confidence in the government.

2. Public financial disclosure will demonstrate the high level of integrity of the vast majority of government officials.

3. Public financial disclosure will deter conflicts of interest from arising.

4. Public financial disclosure will deter some persons who should not be entering public service from doing so.

5. Public financial disclosure will better enable the public to judge the performance of public officials.[26]

In a variety of ways the ethics act also sought to shield public officials from improper influence—by their former colleagues or by interests affected by their decisions and actions. In his call for extensions and enlargements of several of the post-employment restrictions on former government employees, President Carter suggested that such restrictions would "prevent the misuse of influence acquired through public service."[27] The report of the Senate Governmental Affairs Committee elaborated on this concern.

[The post-employment restrictions] have several important objectives. The restrictions are imposed to insure government efficiency, eliminate official corruption, and promote even-handed exercise of administrative discretion. Former officers should not be permitted to exercise undue influence over former colleagues, still in office, in matters pending before the agencies; they should not be permitted to utilize information on specific cases gained during government service for their own benefit and that of private clients. Both are forms of unfair advantage.[28]

One other widely cited goal of the ethics act was the establishment of a management system that would ensure forceful and consistent administration of all ethics regulations. Broad and equally applied requirements would be made for personal financial disclosure with heavy civil penalties for violations and criminal penalties for "knowing or willful" violations. Violators of the post-employment restrictions faced potential jail time. A new federal agency, the Office of Government Ethics (OGE), would supervise the implementation of this program, providing training for agency ethics officers, counsel for government employees, and directives to those with potential conflicts of interest. When persons at the top of the executive branch—the president, vice president, cabinet officers, or White House aides—were charged with violations, the law permitted the appointment of a special prosecutor, an approach that President Carter believed would "eliminate all appearance of high-level interference in sensitive investigations and prosecutions."[29]

A General Accounting Office (GAO) report to Congress in early 1977 had noted several deficiencies in the procedures that then existed for preventing conflicts of interest.[30] First, there was little or no interpretation of standards-of-conduct regulation by individual agencies or much effort to apply general standards to the specific concerns of agency employees. Thus many employees lacked important guidance on how to act in ethically sensitive situations.

Second, agencies were inconsistent in their enforcement of requirements for filing confidential personal financial reports. In some agencies, the GAO found, more than 10 percent of such required reports had not been filed, and in many agencies those reports that were filed were often not carefully reviewed.

Third, the GAO noted many instances of ineffective and untimely resolution of conflicts of interest. Often a year or more would elapse between the filing of a report that indicated a potential conflict and action by the agency to work with the employee in curing it.

These findings convinced many in Congress of the need within the executive branch for "a cohesive infrastructure for enforcement of current statutes, executive orders, and regulations dealing with standards of conduct." "A major and perhaps the most substantial contributing factor to the inadequate performance of the executive branch conflict of interest system," declared the Senate Governmental Affairs Committee, "has been the decided lack of a centralized supervisory authority."[31]

A careful reading of the legislative history of the Ethics in Government Act of 1978 thus reveals its dominant justifications.

—The need for vigorous new rules and procedures to restore the confidence of the American people in the ethical integrity of their government.

—The importance of a far-reaching requirement for government employees to make public disclosure of their personal finances to permit identification and prevention of potential conflicts of interest.

—The necessity of preventing improper influence on government actions through post-employment restrictions on all executive branch employees and extraordinary procedures for investigating charges against high-level executive officials.

—The requirement for a special executive branch agency to ensure consistent and aggressive supervision of the federal government's program of ethics regulation.

—The need for clear and significant sanctions to deter potential violators of these regulations.

Troubles and Doubts

The justifications for the ethics act were sufficiently persuasive to win passage in both houses, and by significant majorities in each: 74-5 in the Senate, 368-30 in the House. But a review of the act's legislative history reveals more than just the sentiments of support that enabled its passage. The debate was also full of expressions of concern, of worries and fears for the consequences and side effects of what would be a set of significant changes in the employment conditions of the federal work force.

PRIVACY. For some members of Congress, the ethics act violated a fundamental principle: the right of American citizens to privacy. Especially repugnant in this regard were the executive branch public financial disclosure requirements in Title II of the bill. Rep. Jack Brooks (D-Texas) pointed out that "the U.S. Congress has on a number of occasions in recent years stood up for the right of our citizens to be protected from the indiscriminate publication of personal information. There is no compelling case at this time to treat career government employees as second class citizens who are to be denied these basic protections."[32] He called his colleagues' attention to an opinion issued earlier in 1978 by U.S. District Court Judge Gerhard Gesell.

> In this immediate post-Watergate period, the view exists that conflicts of interest can be expunged by forcing intimate disclosures from those dealing with or acting for the government. Within limits this may be sound, but we must beware lest excessive zeal in this direction destroy more precious fundamental values. People, even people working for the government, have within reason the right to be left alone.[33]

To some members, the problem was overkill: too much invasion of privacy imposed on too many government employees. "You see, if we go beyond that which is necessary to disclose what the public might legitimately inquire into," argued Rep. Charles E. Wiggins (R-Calif.), "we are simply pandering to curiosity, voyeurism, as it were. I do not characterize pandering to public voyeurism as an important and overriding public interest."[34]

Rep. Carlos J. Moorhead (R-Calif.) thought the public disclosure requirement "far broader, in fact, than can be justified by any 'compelling' or 'overriding' public interest. . . . Far more Government officials and employees are covered by this legislation than is really necessary to assure public confidence."[35]

DETAIL. For some members, the problem with public disclosure went beyond mere invasions of personal privacy. They were troubled as well by the legislation's complex reporting categories. Wiggins argued that, in establishing many categories of value for financial disclosure reporting, Congress was calling for detail that served no purpose. "It is like being a little bit pregnant," Wiggins argued. "If you have a conflict at $50,000, I am not sure your conflict is significantly greater at $75,000 or $100,000 or at $200,000."[36]

"Too much unnecessary detail would be required in the reports," Moorhead complained. "The categories of value in [the ethics legislation] are overly detailed to the point of being ridiculous. . . . This overcategorization will only serve misplaced public curiosity, while certainly giving no more additional evidence with regard to potential conflicts of interest."[37]

REVOLVING DOOR. One of the stated goals of the legislation was to slow the so-called revolving door through which public servants departed the government to take up private sector jobs in which they could profit from the knowledge they gained in government or from the special access (and thus influence) they might have with their former colleagues who remained in government. The task, argued many of the bill's proponents, was to slow or stop the revolving door through which people passed from the private to the public sector, and back.

But to some members, concerns with the potential negative effects of the revolving door were overblown. Three members filed additional views to the House Judiciary Committee's report on the bill, noting especially their disagreement about the post-employment restrictions. "What the postgovernment employment restrictions reflect," they noted, "is an underlying belief that the so-called 'revolving door' is somehow bad for government. But, in most instances, the opposite is actually true."[38]

Rep. Bob Eckhardt (D-Texas) noted on the floor that "the evil is not with respect to the revolving door. . . . Our economy is essentially an enterprise system in which government must know something about business and business something about government. It is not evil that there be an interplay between the two."[39]

RECRUITMENT. Especially worrisome to some of the opponents—and even some of the supporters—of the ethics act was its potential effects on presidential appointees. While the legislation's strongest supporters believed that it enhanced public integrity without diminishing the government's recruiting capability, many other members were not so sure.

The report of the Senate Governmental Affairs Committee tried to calm these qualms.

> Conflict of interest standards must be balanced with the government's objective in attracting experienced and qualified persons to public service. Both are important, and a conflicts policy cannot focus on one to the detriment of the other. There can be no doubt that overly stringent restrictions have a decidedly adverse impact on the government's ability to attract and retain able and experienced persons in federal office.
>
> We have given those considerations very deliberate thought. Indeed, for nearly 18 months, the Committee was involved in a detailed study of federal conflict of interest questions and has issued a report dealing with those issues this past February. We have concluded that the revisions contained in Title V will not adversely affect the attraction of federal office to properly motivated individuals.[40]

But the debate bristled with doubts. The bill, said Rep. Samuel S. Stratton (D-N.Y.), "would make it virtually impossible for us to get any of these young, capable scientific or technical individuals to agree to spend any time in the Defense Department at all, because . . . it would be almost impossible for him to get a job after he left government service if he was henceforth forever banned from any contact with the Defense Department."[41]

Rep. Thomas S. Foley (D-Wash.), a supporter of most of the bill's provisions, worried about the effects of public financial disclosure and the post-employment restrictions.

> If we have any concern about the efficiency and effectiveness of government, let me plead with members to stop this useless and foolish idea that we should bar or discourage from federal service those people who have expertise or special knowledge. We represent [American citizens'] interest poorly by encrusting and encumbering the statutes with disincentives to the exceptionally able appointee. . . . We must appoint able and honorable persons to government without these pointless restrictions.[42]

Rep. Barbara Jordan (D-Texas) called on her colleagues to support an amendment that would allow more freedom for post-employment contacts. "We need to be careful," she argued, "that in the passage of this bill we do not codify mediocrity, that we do not, somehow, enforce a lower standard, or below excellent standard for the people who work in the federal government. It is important that in our exuberance over ethics we do not become so exuberant that we deny to the government the kind of talent, the know-how, and the expertise that the government needs."[43]

Nothing so troubled those who opposed the bill—and many of those who ultimately voted for it—than their uncertainty about its effects on the recruitment of presidential appointees and the retention of senior career civil servants. It was clear to many of them that the bar to federal service had been raised, both by requiring officials to submit to unprecedented invasions of their privacy and by limiting the activities in which they might engage in their careers after government service. Would this keep good people away from public service? No one could be certain, but the potential unintended consequences of this legislation were troubling to many.

No More Watergates?

The editorial commentary that accompanied the passage of the Ethics in Government Act of 1978 was a mixture of praise and dismay. But few of the favorable comments noted one of the peculiar ironies of the bill's contents. Almost none of it was directed at the kinds of crimes and misdeeds that inspired sweeping congressional action on ethics. This may have been a response to Watergate, but little in the bill would have prevented the kinds of activities that composed the Watergate scandal. Watergate was about burglary, cover-ups, lying, and campaign irregularities. Nothing in the Ethics in Government Act of 1978 would have added new deterrents to, or punishments for, those behaviors. The ethics act sought to restore public confidence in government after Watergate by creating an array of new regulations that bore little relation to the scandal that inspired them.

As Rep. James M. Collins (R-Texas) noted on the House floor:

> I think this bill is going to be one of the most unfortunate pieces of legislation we pass this year. It is misdirected. . . . We are talking about the ethics bill and it comes basically from three background situations. One of them is Watergate. . . .
>
> Watergate, what was that? That was one political party trying to put an electronic bug in another political party's ceiling, and they did not succeed. What has that got to do with an ethics bill?[44]

Living with the New Regulations

President Carter was nearing the end of his term when the ethics act took effect in July 1979. As often occurs in the last eighteen months of a presidential term, the flow of appointments slowed. For Carter aides involved in the appointment process and working in the White House Counsel's office—the principal points of engagement with the requirements of the ethics act—the impact was minimal. Carter had already set standards for his appointees that in many ways matched or exceeded the requirements of the new law, so recruiting was little changed. The White House's principal adjustment was to the use of the new forms and procedures required by the act and to some potential retention problems caused by its stringent post-employment restrictions.

Michael Cardozo, who was deputy counsel to the president, noted the new burdens those forms and procedures imposed: "The process of filling in a form for the White House, filling in a different form, 278, for the agency and for the Office of Government Ethics, and then going through the whole damn thing again with a different form for the Senate committee is cumbersome, far too time consuming, and it ought to be streamlined."[45]

Cardozo cited the example of one wealthy Carter appointee. In complying with the public financial disclosure requirements, he "used Cravath or some other large New York firm to assist him and told me that it had cost him more in legal fees to complete the forms than he would earn in his first year in government."[46]

R. James Woolsey, who served as undersecretary of the Navy in the Carter administration, noted the significant retention and recruiting effects encountered when people in the Defense Department began to contemplate the impact of the post-employment restrictions, especially Section 207(b)(ii) prohibiting former government employees from advising and assisting clients or employers in representation before their former agencies. To many in government or being recruited to serve in government, that restriction would severely hamper their ability to make a living after government.

"With respect to trying to recruit replacements for people who were leaving and also to stem the tide of early retirements which were being contemplated in the winter of 78–79 and down to the spring of 1979, that provision was far and away the most troubling," noted Woolsey. That provision was modified by congressional action before the effective date of the ethics act. Had it not been, Woolsey notes, "I believe not only people in Defense but in HEW, doctors at NIH, e.g., and all of the other people who were seriously concerned about that so-called 'advise and assist' clause would, many of them, no longer be with us and we would have virtually no chance of getting others to replace them."[47]

John L. Moore, who served as counsel on conflicts of interest during the Carter transition and later as chairman of the board of directors of the Export-Import Bank, did not find the specific requirements of the ethics act a substantial impediment to presidential recruiting. But he came to believe that the ethics act in less direct ways weakened the appeal of public service. "The overall atmosphere," he noted, "has become awfully demeaning. . . . It may be more important in deterring people concerning government service than some of the technical aspects of whether you actually have to disclose or fill out three forms instead of two. I would certainly like to see some better attitude."[48]

Adjustments to the ethics act in the Carter administration were simplified by several factors. One was the administration's strong support for the act; it was, after all, Jimmy Carter who had proposed it after making a "return to high ethical standards" and "a government you can trust" the hallmarks of his campaign for the presidency. But there were other facilitating factors as well. The ethics act took effect at a time in the Carter administration when its procedures for recruiting and processing presidential appointees had been tested and refined, and at a point in the life of the administration when the flow of appointments was relatively light. The people who had to adjust to the daily impacts of the new legislation knew what they were doing and what to expect. In addition, the administration appointed the head of the new Office of Government Ethics, J. Jackson Walter, and it worked closely with him in bringing the act on line. There were few surprises and little tension.

This was not so after Ronald Reagan's election in 1980. The first presidential transition under the new ethics rules took place after that election. In many ways, the Reagan staff had done a better job of preparing for the personnel selection task that a new president faces than any of its predecessors. A transition planning office had begun operating in Alexandria, Virginia, in July 1980 and was ready to begin recommending candidates for appointment on the day after the election.

Except for one thing: E. Pendleton James, who headed the Reagan transition planning operation, had not worked in government since the Nixon administration and was unfamiliar with the ethics act. The transition personnel planning proceeded without any provisions for a process to comply with the reporting requirements of the act. The Office of Government Ethics had prepared an extensive set of briefing papers for the new administration, which Walter at OGE recalls handing to James directly.[49] And White House aides in the outgoing Carter administration were prepared to provide guidance to the new administration as well. But, as often happens during presidential transitions, the incoming people have little time or desire to meet with the people they were replacing. James and his personnel team were trying to cope with the need to find suitable candidates to fill hundreds of positions. The details of the appointment process compelled little of their attention—until the time came to start nominating Ronald Reagan's team.[50]

"That's when I became aware of the Ethics in Government Act of 1978," said James. "In spite of all the planning, I had overlooked the Act, overlooked it because I frankly wasn't aware of the extent that it would affect our appointments."[51] The process, which had started with such promise, soon slowed precipitously. Complaints arose from the administration's supporters, wondering where were the nominees. "It wasn't that we weren't finding candidates, but we found that it took almost three to four months to process the paperwork before we could send names to the Hill for confirmation. . . . The Ethics in Government Act require[d] us to spend an inordinate amount of time complying with it before your name can go up."[52]

The Reagan administration drew many of its appointees from business, especially from the world of large corporations. For many of them, Washington was a kind of culture shock, and compliance with the Ethics in Government Act was their first confrontation with this new and often alien culture. No small number of those invited to serve in the Reagan administration declined the honor. A "disappointing number of outstanding candidates for high government positions decline to serve," James wrote in April 1982, and the "chief obstacle at present is the Ethics in Government Act."[53]

Fred Fielding, who was President Reagan's counsel during the early years of the administration, echoed this concern about the cumulative impact of the ethics act on recruiting. "From our experience," he said, "in a significant number of cases, talented individuals who are otherwise willing to serve, even at considerable financial sacrifice, have concluded that the price of a detailed public disclosure of one's private affairs is simply too high a price to pay, especially when combined with all the other requirements of coming into public service."[54]

The recruitment effects and the difficulties in getting appointees in place and on the job were felt by Reagan's cabinet officers as well. Terrel H. Bell, who came to Washington as secretary of education, reflected on the burden the ethics requirements imposed on his own efforts to recruit a team of leaders for his department: "Many outstanding citizens would be willing to respond to a call from the president or from a Cabinet officer to serve their country, but they are understandably unwilling to run the gamut of this procedure. The nation loses many of its best qualified potential public servants because of this lengthy and excruciating process of public exposure."[55]

Those appointees who did accept President Reagan's invitation to serve often found that the ethics act required some significant alterations in their personal finances. A study conducted in 1985 of appointees serving after June 1979, most of whom were first-term Reagan appointees, found that more than two-thirds were required to rearrange their personal finances or file recusal statements to comply with the ethics laws. Table 3-2 indicates the variety of actions they undertook.

Correcting Course

The Ethics in Government Act only began the process of constructing a framework of ethics regulation for the federal government. Tinkering with the language of the act has been almost constant since 1978.

Table 3-2. *Compliance Actions Required of Administration Appointees Serving between July 1979 and December 1984*

Compliance action	Percent of appointees
No action required	32.8
Created blind or diversified trust	13.1
Sold stock or other assets	32.3
Resigned positions in corporations or other organizations	40.9
Executed recusal statement	16.7

Source: National Academy of Public Administration, Presidential Appointee Project. Data on Reagan administration appointees are drawn from a survey of all living presidential appointees who served at Executive Level IV or above from 1964 to 1984.

The Ethics in Government Act was scheduled to go into effect on July 1, 1979. But even before its effective date, problems arose. Numerous high-ranking officials in the executive branch threatened to resign before the effective date to avoid the act's strict limitations on post-employment activity. And the Carter administration was beginning to experience some resistance in its efforts to recruit presidential appointees because of those limitations.[56]

At the strong urging of the president, Congress quickly passed a bill that softened several features of the post-employment provisions before they ever took effect.[57] The ethics act imposed a two-year ban on former government employees "assisting in representing" their private employers before their former agencies, which the new law specified as personal appearances. Other forms of assistance and advice would not be prohibited. This two-year ban was also limited only to matters on which the former employee had participated "personally and substantially" while in government. The new law also exempted from many of the post-employment provisions those former government employees who went to work for colleges and universities, medical research and treatment institutions, or state and local governments.

During the debate on the bill in the House Judiciary Committee, Republicans launched an assault on the entire ethics act for being, as one of them argued, "far too broad in scope, too extensive, too punitive."[58] An amendment proposed in committee by Rep. Robert McClory (R-Ill.) to impose a six-month moratorium on the effective date of the ethics act to permit a thorough study of the law was defeated by a 12-16 vote.

Rethinking the Special Prosecutor

The special prosecutor provision of the ethics act was scheduled to expire on October 1, 1983.[59] In 1982 Congress enacted legislation that revised that provision and extended it for five years. President Reagan signed the extension, but his administration had opposed it during congressional consideration. The Justice Department had argued that it had the capability to investigate and prosecute the kinds of crimes covered by the special prosecutor provision and it was, therefore, unnecessary.

The special prosecutor procedures had been initiated eleven times between 1978 and the end of 1982. In only three of those cases had a special prosecutor been appointed to investigate. Two of them involved allegations of illegal drug use by Hamilton Jordan, President Carter's chief of staff, and Tim Kraft, the manager of the Carter-Mondale Presidential Committee. In neither case was there sufficient evidence to warrant a prosecution, despite lengthy and expensive investigations. The investigation of Hamilton Jordan, for example, cost $215,621.[60]

The third appointment of a special prosecutor was for the investigation of Reagan labor secretary Raymond J. Donovan for alleged corrupt practices before he entered government. Here, too, the special prosecutor, Leon Silverman, found insufficient evidence to prosecute. In each of the other eight cases in which a special prosecutor investigation had been sought, the attorney general had conducted a preliminary investigation and found no cause to appoint a special prosecutor.

In renewing this approach for five years, Congress made several changes. It changed the name of the special prosecutor to "independent counsel." It raised the standard for triggering the appointment of an independent counsel. And it added several other provisions that narrowed the coverage of the independent counsel procedure. But the independent counsel survived.

OGE out from Under

A year later, in 1983, the Office of Government Ethics came up for renewal after five years in existence. In extending OGE for another five years, Congress made several changes. It broadened the independence of the office by granting it its own budget line and authorizing it to issue rules and regulations. It gave the director a five-year term and wider capacity to deal with agency ethics officers and inspectors general. Congress also used the opportunity provided by this renewal to make other changes in the basic ethics law—limiting the outside earned income of senior White House aides and altering some of the technical details of financial disclosure procedures, blind trusts, and formal ethics agreements undertaken by officials to cure potential conflicts of interest.[61]

In the subsequent five-year reviews of the independent counsel law and OGE reauthorization, the tinkering continued.[62] The scope of the independent counsel's authority was broadened. So, too, was the independence of OGE and the breadth of its authority in dealing with departments and agencies. The pattern was becoming clearer now that each of these periodic reauthorizations afforded Congress an opportunity to review the operations of the ethics network and revise it or add new dimensions to cope with problems that occurred in practice. For example, Attorney General Edwin Meese III had declined to appoint an independent counsel to investigate charges that U.S. ambassador to Switzerland Faith Ryan Whittlesey had misused government funds. Meese did not believe that Whittlesey had demonstrated any criminal intent. In the 1987 extension of the independent counsel law, however, new provisions were added that prohibited the attorney general from considering an accused official's state of mind when deciding whether to appoint an independent counsel.

Step Aside for Mr. Clean

The election of George H. W. Bush in 1988 set off a new round of ethics regulations. Bush's Democratic opponent, Massachusetts governor Michael S. Dukakis, had made the ethics of the Reagan-Bush administration a focus of his campaign attacks. In their second campaign debate, Dukais said, "Integrity is not a Republican or a Democratic issue; it's an American issue. . . . We've had dozens and dozens of officials in this administration who have left under a cloud, who have left with the special prosecutor in their arm, have been indicted, convicted. This isn't the kind of administration we need."[63]

While Bush offered an awkward defense of the Reagan era ethics during the campaign, he hastened to distance himself from his predecessor on this issue when it was over. Bush appointed the President's Commission on the Federal Appointment Process to examine existing ethics regulations and recommend changes. He also issued Executive Order 12674, which identified a set of ethical principles for government officers and employees and added a specific proscription that went beyond the ethics statutes to impose a total ban on outside earned income for presidential appointees. In the second campaign debate in 1988, Vice President Bush was asked, "Will you lock that revolving door that has allowed some men and women in government to come back and lobby the very departments they once managed?"

"Yes, and I'll apply it to Congress, too. I'll do both," Bush replied. "Look, we need the highest possible ethical standards. I will have an ethical office in the White House that will be under the president's personal concern. . . . But there is no corner on this sleaze factor, believe me. And it's a disgrace, and I will do my level best to clean it up."[64]

President Bush made several proposals that Congress soon took up. Later that year it passed the Ethics Reform Act of 1989.[65] The act broadened post-employment restrictions to cover a wider range of federal employees and to include specific bans on representing foreign governments or seeking to influence trade or treaty negotiations. It expanded the coverage of the financial disclosure requirements and increased the complexity of the reporting categories. It tightened gift acceptance rules and restrictions on subsidized travel. All federal employees were barred from receiving honoraria for any purpose while employed by the government, and senior federal employees could earn no more than 15 percent of Executive Level II salaries in outside earned income.

The provisions of this act took ethics regulations in a number of new directions. The act also inspired a strong and angry reaction: retirements and threatened retirements in many agencies before its effective date, lawsuits from federal employee unions, and immediate calls for amendment from unhappy members of Congress.[66]

One Up

President-elect Bill Clinton followed what had become the normal course by beginning his administration with the announcement of ethics standards more stringent than those required by law or those followed by any other president. On December 9, 1992, one day before Clinton announced his first cabinet choice, his transition director, Warren M. Christopher, held a press conference in Little Rock, Arkansas, and said that all Clinton nominees would be asked to sign a contract in which they pledged to refrain from lobbying their former agencies for five years after leaving government service and pledged never to represent foreign governments or foreign political parties on any matter before the U.S. government.[67] By requiring each nominee to sign a contractually binding pledge, Christopher believed the administration could seek a court injunction against any future violators.

In announcing this more restrictive ban on post-employment activities, Christopher said, "It's a matter of . . . preventing any possible vice that's inherent in the system as it now exists." He called the action "just the beginning of Gov. Clinton's efforts to give the government back to the people."[68]

A majority of the presidents who had come to office since 1961 had similarly taken actions to emphasize the commitment of their administrations to the highest standards of public integrity. This recurring game of ethical leapfrog had a significant long-term cumulative effect. It resulted not only in ever more restrictive standards of conduct for presidential appointees, but it also put an implicit burden on each new administration to act before or quickly after taking office—and certainly before it had had an opportunity to determine the likely impact of its new standards on recruitment and retention of presidential appointees. This was a most peculiar form of policymaking: announcing solutions before experiencing or studying the problems—and before understanding the consequences.[69]

The New Politics of Government Ethics, 1961–2000

The construction of current ethics policies was the product of steady, piecemeal accumulation over several decades. Few areas of policy in modern history have been so constantly tinkered with and revised. Most presidential administrations and many of the Congresses since 1961 have made a contribution.

The Character of Policymaking

This policymaking process and the political dynamics that energized it are distinctive in several ways. In public policymaking, it is common for problems to come to the attention of the public, to work their way onto the public agenda, and then to be carefully assessed by experts who yield a variety of options for policy consideration. Policy analyses identify those approaches most likely to be effective and efficient responses to the problems. This is normally followed by extensive debate within political institutions in which many voices are heard. Such debate is then followed by efforts at consensus building, which may or may not yield majorities in support of new policy initiatives designed to address the problems that inspired the initial concerns.

But the ongoing debate over ethics policies little resembles the normal model. Most of the ethics policies initiated over the past four decades were inspired not by careful policy evaluation in which problems were analyzed and known or tested solutions applied or costs and benefits measured and carefully weighed. They were inspired instead largely by the efforts of legislators to offer a dramatic response to the scandal of the moment and by presidents to distance themselves from the ethical imbroglios of their predecessors. In both branches, the highest objective seemed to be to win political credit for raising ethical standards to new plateaus. That those higher standards might yield no significant improvement in government integrity, or that they might have negative side effects or consequences, was rarely a prominent consideration in these debates. The bottom line was infrequently in sight because there was so little calculation of costs and benefits. Visibility often seemed more important than viability.

So it was a peculiar form of policymaking in which new policies often bore little direct relation—and offered little direct response or corrective—to the problems that inspired them. Many of those problems already had solutions embedded in law, and no further regulation was necessary. Watergate is a good example. In Watergate, the system worked. Lawbreakers went to jail. Officials who lost the confidence of Congress or the people left the government. A president was driven from office. Little in the post-Watergate ethics regulations improved the capacity of the legal or political system to deter, detect, or punish the misbehavior that constituted the Watergate scandals.[70]

But that reality was rarely recognized and never articulated by those caught up in the spirit of "no more Watergates." "The temptation to rectify lawbreaking with more law was irresistible," writes Stanley L. Kutler in his comprehensive history of Watergate.[71]

> When the expectation of executive virtue is disappointed, the weight of such disappointment almost inevitably produces a massive response which, however naively, attempts to ensure against any repetition of executive offenses. Some of the resulting measures succeed; some amount to little more than an exercise in futility or wrongheadedness.[72]

Also noteworthy about the politics of ethics policymaking was the absence of any identifiable public demand for most of the new components of that policy. Public trust in government and public perceptions of the honesty of government officials were in steady decline during this forty-year period. A broad and ambiguous public unhappiness with government was manifest. But there was never a public clamor for any of the specific approaches that were ultimately codified and institutionalized in ethics regulations. No lawmaker won a seat or lost a seat in Congress by calling for more ethics legislation or by silence on the issue. To the extent that the American people communicated any message at all on the issue of government ethics, they seemed to want only better behavior from their leaders. There was no public clamor for more law, only for more adherence to law.

The debate over these new regulations, when it occurred at all, was also notable for the wheels that did not squeak. Much of the new regulatory policy resulted from executive orders, most commonly issued at the outset of a president's term—that is, before there was much opportunity for the complex challenges of recruiting and retention to be fully experienced and understood by new administrations. There is little to indicate that presidents heard at all from those who would be directly affected by the regulations they ordered or that they carefully considered the constraints such orders would impose on their own recruiters.

When Congress passed ethics laws, no one effectively articulated the concerns of current or potential presidential appointees. No one asked for advice from the incumbents or veterans in those jobs, and the future had no spokesperson. Only a relatively small number of members of Congress worried about the potentially harmful impacts of these regulations, raised doubts, or offered opposition. But they were usually steamrollered by the relentless momentum for "more ethics" and by the worrisome political consequence of opposing any legislation that seemed to promise "more ethics."

CHAPTER FOUR

The
Tightened Net

The accumulated product of four decades of ethics rule-making, layered on top of the basic conflict-of-interest and abuse-of-office statutes, is a tightly woven regulatory net designed to trap every form and every instance of misbehavior by federal employees. What are the characteristics of the policies for regulating the ethics of individuals who serve in the federal government?

The focus of discussion here is limited to those regulations that deal with conflict of interest and abuse of office in the executive branch. No attention is given to the regulation of campaign finance; the political activities of career employees governed by the Hatch Act; prohibited personnel practices regulated by the Office of Personnel Management (OPM), the Merit Systems Protection Board (MSPB), or Equal Employment Opportunity Commission; the ethics regulations that apply to members of Congress or the judiciary; or the vast array of ethics regulations at the state and local level that mirror, and sometimes go beyond, federal policies. All of those would be rich lodes of research, but they are outside the scope of this analysis.

The Regulations

Several theories underlay federal ethics regulation. Primary among those is the notion that education and training are essential to alert federal employees to the ethical vexations inherent in their work and to their obligations to avoid conflicts of interest or abuse of office.

Education and Training

Ethics education for federal employees starts with the statement of ethical responsibilities included in what is usually called the federal Code of Ethics. In fact, many federal codes over more than a century have led up to the current "Fourteen Principles of Ethical Conduct for Federal Employees" (see box 4-1). This statement of first principles is the starting point for ethics education. It hangs in most federal workplaces, and all federal employees are exposed to it at the outset of their federal service.

But the code is just a small part of the training and education effort that underlies ethics regulation. The Office of Government Ethics (OGE) and each of the agencies and departments conduct regular training sessions and engage in a variety of other initiatives aimed at reminding federal employees of their ethical responsibilities and explaining the substance of those responsibilities.

Each agency and department has its own ethics officer, the designated agency ethics official (DAEO), who works closely with OGE in developing materials and training sessions tailored to the specific needs and duties of the agency. The DAEOs themselves are offered regular training and receive periodic DAEOgrams from OGE with information about new materials, changes in rules or law, and interpretations of ethics rules in specific cases. This training function occurs beyond public view for the most part, but it is a central day-to-day component of ethics regulation.

Financial Disclosure

Keeping federal employees out of trouble is a primary goal of ethics policy. Amy Comstock, director of the Office of Government Ethics, noted about many of the ethics statutes:

> They are prophylactic. They keep people from having to decide am I doing the right thing, am I sure I'm not making a decision just because I own stock in a company. In fact, what they do is prohibit the employee from participating at all. They keep the federal employee from having to determine the right thing or struggle to do the right thing. . . .
>
> What we do is, through a process of financial disclosure, we review someone's holdings and assets to determine if we think they will have a conflict of interest.[1]

Box 4-1. *Fourteen Principles of Ethical Conduct for Federal Employees*

(1) Public service is a public trust, requiring employees to place loyalty to the Constitution, the laws and ethical principles above private gain.

(2) Employees shall not hold financial interests that conflict with the conscientious performance of duty.

(3) Employees shall not engage in financial transactions using nonpublic government information or allow the improper use of such information to further any private interest.

(4) An employee shall not, except as permitted by the Standards of Ethical Conduct, solicit or accept any gift or other item of monetary value from any person or entity seeking official action from, doing business with, or conducting activities regulated by the employee's agency, or whose interests may be substantially affected by the performance or nonperformance of the employee's duties.

(5) Employees shall put forth honest effort in the performance of their duties.

(6) Employees shall not knowingly make unauthorized commitments or promises of any kind purporting to bind the Government.

(7) Employees shall not use public office for private gain.

(8) Employees shall act impartially and not give preferential treatment to any private organization or individual.

(9) Employees shall protect and conserve federal property and shall not use it for other than authorized activities.

(10) Employees shall not engage in outside employment or activities, including seeking or negotiating for employment, that conflict with official government duties and responsibilities.

(11) Employees shall disclose waste, fraud, abuse, and corruption to appropriate authorities.

(12) Employees shall satisfy in good faith their obligations as citizens, including all financial obligations, especially those-such as federal, state, or local taxes-that are imposed by law.

(13) Employees shall adhere to all laws and regulations that provide equal opportunity for all Americans regardless of race, color, religion, sex, national origin, age, or handicap.

(14) Employees shall endeavor to avoid any actions creating the appearance that they are violating the law or the ethical standards set forth in the Standards of Ethical Conduct. Whether particular circumstances create an appearance that the law or these standards have been violated shall be determined from the perspective of a reasonable person with knowledge of the relevant facts.

Source: U.S. Office of Government Ethics, *Do It Right: An Ethics Handbook for Executive Branch Employees* (Government Printing Office, 1995).

Table 4-1. *Financial Disclosure Forms Filed, 1995–2000*

Year	SF-278 (public)	OGE-450 (confidential)
1995	21,019	262,138
1996	21,509	272,925
1997	21,205	264,241
1998	20,516	262,987
1999	20,892	259,209
2000	20,975	251,326
Average	21,019	262,138
Total	126,116	1,572,826

Source: Calculated from data provided by the U.S. Office of Government Ethics.

More than 280,000 executive branch employees are required to make annual disclosure of their personal finances. Approximately 21,000 of those are required to make public disclosure. The number of filers in each category between 1995 and 2000 is in table 4-1. The principal categories of people required to make public disclosure are indicated in box 4-2.

Employees required to make public financial disclosure do so on Standard Form 278, which is a complex instrument with eleven pages of instructions. Filers must place the value of their assets in one of twelve categories of value and their sources of income in one of eleven categories of value. Confidential filers use OGE Form 450. These are filed each year with their agency's DAEO.

Disclosure, whether public or confidential, is intended to be the first step in a process of consultation between the employee and an appropriate ethics official. During this consultation, any assets, memberships, and so on that pose a potential conflict of interest should be identified. The employee and the ethics officials should then agree on an appropriate cure (divestiture, recusal, waiver, and so on) to ensure that the potential conflict is mitigated.

OGE director Comstock described this process as "prophylactic." Its purpose is to identify the potential for conflict of interest and cure it before a conflict arises in practice. If federal employees can be isolated from any circumstances in which they might face a conflict of interest, the theory holds, then the employees will have little opportunity to put their personal financial interests before their larger public responsibilities in making government decisions.

Box 4-2. *Federal Employees Required to Make Annual Public Financial Disclosure*

a. Candidates for nomination or election to the office of President or Vice President.

b. Presidential nominees to positions requiring the advice and consent of the Senate, other than those nominated for judicial office or as a Foreign Service Officer or for appointment to a rank in the uniformed services at a pay grade of O-6, or below.

c. The following newly elected or appointed officials:
  • The President;
  • The Vice President;
  • Officers and employees (including special Government employees, as defined in 18 U.S.C. § 202) whose positions are classified above GS-15 of the General Schedule, or the rate of basic pay for which is fixed, other than under the General Schedule, at a rate equal to or greater than 120% of the minimum rate of basic pay for GS-15 of the General Schedule.
  • Members of the uniformed services in pay grade O-7 or above;
  • Officers or employees in any other positions determined by the Director of the Office of Government Ethics to be of equal classification to above GS-15;
  • Administrative law judges;
  • Employees in the excepted service in positions which are of a confidential or policy-making character, unless by regulation their positions have been excluded by the Director of the Office of Government Ethics;
  • The Postmaster General, the Deputy Postmaster General, each Governor of the Board of Governors of the U.S. Postal Service and officers or employees of the U.S. Postal Service or Postal Rate Commission in positions for which the rate of basic pay is equal to or greater than 120% of the minimum rate of basic pay for GS-15 of the General Schedule;
  • The Director of the Office of Government Ethics and each designated agency ethics official; and
  • Civilian employees in the Executive Office of the President (other than special Government employees) who hold commissions of appointment from the President.

d. Incumbent officials holding positions referred to in section II.c. of these instructions if they have served 61 days or more in the position during the preceding calendar year.

e. Officials who have terminated employment after having served 61 days or more in a calendar year in a position referred to in section II.c. and have not accepted another such position within 30 days thereafter.

Source: Executive Personnel Financial Disclosure Report (SF-278).

Conflict of Interest

What is a prohibited conflict of interest? A criminal statute prohibits a federal employee from participating in a particular matter in which, to his knowledge, he has a financial interest.[2] It must be a situation in which a decision has a direct and predictable effect on the employee's financial interests.

For example, a federal employee who owns stock in a company that sells office supplies would have a conflict of interest if she participated in a decision to award a contract to that company to provide supplies for her agency. Under current interpretation of law, she would also have a conflict if her spouse or minor child worked for the company or had a financial interest in the company, even if she did not. And she would have a potential conflict if she were negotiating with the company for future employment while still in government service.

In any of those cases, she would be obliged to declare the potential conflict of interest and avoid participation in the contract decision or seek a waiver from the appropriate ethics officer that allowed her to participate in the decision—perhaps because her interest was so small or remote. If the employee were in one of the categories of personnel required to make public or confidential disclosure of her personal finances, the interest in the company would have been identified at that time and the appropriate cure designed.

Using Public Office for Private Gain

Several regulations, some of them very long-standing criminal laws, discourage federal employees from profiting from their public service. The most obvious of these are the bribery laws that prohibit public actions in exchange for private compensation—the classic quid pro quo arrangement.[3]

Federal employees must also avoid the exercise of undue influence. This occurs when a government employee with a private financial interest, but no capacity to make decisions to benefit that interest, tries to influence another government official who has the necessary capacity to act in favor of the interest. For example, an Internal Revenue Service (IRS) auditor whose spouse is an executive of a private company may have no direct role in a tax audit of that company but might try to influence the auditor assigned to the company to go easy in the audit. Such undue influence has long been barred.[4]

Employees must also avoid taking advantage of the prestige or authority of their public office or the knowledge it provides them for private gain. The range of possibilities here is endless: using government stationery to encourage a bank to make a loan to an employee's child, endorsing a consumer product using one's government title, receiving an honorarium for a speech in which a government employee described the findings of a government study, and so on.

Federal statutes have also long prohibited supplementation of salary.[5] Federal employees may not receive compensation for the performance of their public responsibilities from anyone other than the government. Suppose, for example, that a National Aeronautics and Space Administration computer specialist with children in college were contemplating leaving government for a higher-paying job in the private sector. She has been working on a major programming breakthrough that will significantly accelerate the turnaround time for space shuttle missions. Her supervisor, hoping to keep her on the job, contacts a private foundation that wants to support government innovation and the foundation offers to provide her $20,000 a year for two years if she will stay in government to finish the project on which she is working. A creative approach to personnel management perhaps, but it would constitute an illegal supplementation of salary.

Representation of Private Citizens

Federal law since the Civil War has banned the practice of government employees representing private citizens or private interests in any claim pending before the government.[6] This broad proscription applies even to claims in areas in which the federal employee has no jurisdiction. It also does not matter whether the government employee is compensated for this kind of representation or if it takes place on the personal time of the government employee. Under none of those conditions may a federal employee represent anyone in a claim before the federal government. For example, an Environmental Protection Agency employee could not represent a private citizen making a claim for larger veteran's benefits.

Federal employees may not even assist indirectly in the preparation or making of a claim against the government. The only exceptions to this prohibition are those that allow federal employees to participate in claims made by members of their own family or when a federal employee gives testimony under oath. Employees may not, however, serve as expert witnesses for a private party in any proceeding before a court or agency of the United States if the United States is a party or has a direct and substantial interest.

Gifts

All federal employees face detailed restrictions on the receipt of gifts.[7] No gift may be accepted from any person or organization that seeks any action or decision from the employee's agency, does business or seeks to do business with the agency, is regulated by the agency, has interests that may be substantially affected by the way the employee performs his or her duties, or gives the gift because of the employee's official position.

Because many federal employees interact closely and regularly with such people and organizations, and meals or exchanges of items of only inciden- tal value are a normal part of such interaction, there are some exceptions to the gift prohibitions. These include modest refreshments (coffee, donuts, and so on) not offered as part of a meal, greeting cards, plaques and tro- phies, anything for which the government employee pays market value, and noncash gifts worth less than $20.[8]

Despite this limited list of exceptions, the general gift rule is clear and stark. Federal employees may not accept any gift of consequence from any person or organization that might be affected by the employee's official actions or those of his or her agency. If a Federal Aviation Administration employee were invited to address a conference of airline executives to dis- cuss new security practices in baggage handling, for example, and upon arriving at the conference hotel found a bottle of good champagne and show tickets worth $200 waiting in his room as an expression of gratitude for his attendance, that employee could not accept those gifts.

Outside Employment and Activities

While federal employees are free to engage in a wide range of activities outside their jobs, there are some important restrictions. For example, a fed- eral employee may not be a member of a private organization when such membership might require disqualification from participation in official responsibilities and thus materially impair the employee's performance of his duty. An employee of the National Endowment of the Arts who partici- pates in grant decisions affecting dance companies may not join an organi- zation that sponsors the development of modern dance, for example.

A federal employee may teach, give speeches, or write articles, but he may not be compensated for any of these activities if the subject of his teaching, speaking, or writing is part of his official duties; the invitation to teach, speak, or write was extended primarily because of the employee's official position or because the employee is in a position to help the organization that extended the invitation to teach, speak, or write; or the activity draws substantially on nonpublic information or deals in significant part with the agency's activities and policies.

A federal employee who is a professional accountant, for example, may teach an introductory accounting course at a local community college to earn some extra money. But that employee may not use her federal title in any of the advertising for the course, may not use discussions of the policies and programs of her agency or her specific job assignments as a significant part of the course, and may not use information she learned in her job that is not readily available to the public.

Outside Income

The income that federal employees earn from sources other than the government has long been a subject of concern and restriction by ethics laws. The most important of these is the proscription on supplementation of salary.[9] First enacted in 1917, the supplementation ban restricts federal employees from receiving anything other than their government salary as compensation for the performance of their public duties. They may not receive additional compensation from any private interest, including corporations, organizations, foundations, or individuals.

If a foundation wanted to award a grant to a federal employee at the National Institutes of Health to support his cancer research and the grant included a personal stipend for the employee, it would violate the supplementation of salary rule. If a wealthy philanthropist wanted to supplement the salary of a distinguished federal prosecutor to permit the prosecutor to stay in public service, the prosecutor would not be allowed to accept the supplement even if the philanthropist had no business or interest before the government that might pose a conflict of interest.

May federal employees then earn outside income for matters not related to their official duties? This has been a matter in hot dispute in recent years. For most of American history, federal employees at all levels were permitted to engage in income-producing activities outside their official duties, so long as there was no conflict between the two. That began to change in the 1960s, as new laws and executive orders began to shrink the kinds of activities in which employees might engage and to impose limits on the amounts they could earn beyond their government salaries.[10]

In April 1989, President George H. W. Bush issued Executive Order 12674, which banned all outside earned income for presidential appointees to full-time positions. Later that year, the Ethics Reform Act of 1989 limited the outside earned income of other noncareer officials paid in excess of the GS-15 level to 15 percent of the annual rate of basic pay for Level II of the Executive Schedule in any calendar year.[11]

That law also prohibited all federal employees from receiving honoraria, even for activities that had nothing to do with their government duties. This was the famous (though apocryphal) "beekeeper" restriction, which barred a federal employee who kept bees as a hobby from receiving an honorarium for a speech at the beekeepers' convention.

The ban angered career federal employees, and one of their unions sued to have it overturned. In 1995, in the case of *National Treasury Employees Union v. United States*, the Supreme Court struck down the portion of the honorarium ban that applied to career federal employees, declaring it a violation of their First Amendment rights.[12] When the dust from this case had settled, the following restrictions on outside earned income remained in place: Presidential appointees may not receive any outside income during their presidential appointments, and other noncareer officials paid in excess of the GS-15 level may earn no more outside income in a calendar year than 15 percent of the base salary of Executive Level II. In addition, a number of prohibitions were put on the sources and kinds of activities from which such outside income may be earned.[13]

The beekeeper is back in business—unless he is a presidential appointee.

Misuse of Office

Federal employees confront abundant temptations to use their positions for inappropriate purposes. In some cases, these temptations are common in nearly all work environments: using the office equipment for personal matters, initiating expensive office redecorations, using the company car for personal shopping, and so on. But government employees also face temptations that are unique to their environment.

One of those is using their government authority to accomplish non-public purposes. For example, an employee of the Justice Department might write a law school recommendation for a neighbor's child on official Justice Department stationery. Or an employee of the Federal Communications Commission might identify her official position in trying to get lower long-distance rates for her home phone. Those are misuses of office.

Federal employees are also restricted in the way they use information they obtain through their official work.[14] Federal statutes bar the use or disclosure of confidential and inside information. An employee of the Occupational Safety and Health Administration who knows that a company is about to be socked with a large fine for violating workplace safety standards would be misusing her office if she warned her sister to sell her stock in that company before the information became public.

Another restriction is on the misuse of government property. Such property may not be used for private purposes or "for other than officially approved activities."[15] The Coast Guard employee who takes his friends for a ride on a boat seized from a drug smuggler or the Census Bureau employee who takes her government computer home for her son to use in writing his term paper are both guilty of this kind of misuse of office.

Federal employees are similarly barred from directing their subordinates to engage in activities that do not relate to their public duties. A government secretary, for example, may not be asked to use government time to type a novel that her boss has written on his own time. Nor may the boss use government time to write the novel or engage in any other activity that is not related to his official duties. Official time must be used for official purposes.

While misuse of office is a category that covers a wide array of activity, the core principle is simple. Employees should draw and observe a very bright line separating their official duties and the resources that come with them from their personal lives.

Post-Employment Activities

The activities in which former federal employees engage after leaving federal service began to draw the attention of ethics regulators during World War I. Their concerns grew out of the practice of War Department officials leaving the government, obtaining employment with military contractors, then using information they gained in government to give their new employers unfair advantages in the competition for contracts.

In 1919 Congress enacted restrictions on War Department employees engaged in procurement activities, prohibiting the use of inside information to help private entities to seek military contracts. The ban would last for two years after the employee left government service, but it applied only to those who had served in the executive branch during World War I.

In later years, the regulation of post-employment activities became a more common target of those seeking to expand the regulatory net. But the major expansion occurred as part of the Ethics in Government Act of 1978, which established the basic post-employment standards. Those have been amended on several occasions since then.

The post-employment rules are guided by several basic principles. First, former government employees should not use information or contacts gained from government service to provide unfair advantage to private parties making claims against or seeking business with the government. Second, former employees should not switch sides after leaving government. Third, participating in any decision or activity that involves a prospective employer is a conflict of interest for an employee planning to leave government.

SWITCHING SIDES. A lifetime ban has been imposed against acting as a representative on "particular matters" in which an individual "personally and substantially" participated as a government employee.[16] This is the primary ban on switching sides. The prohibition applies to all former government employees, regardless of rank, but it is limited to particular matters in which the legal rights of specific parties are involved. The former government employee need not be paid for services to a private client or employer to trigger this ban; the prohibition applies even to uncompensated representation.

The lifetime ban does not apply when the former employee was involved only in general program design or rule-making. The emphasis here is on "particular" matters. For example, a former employee of the Comptroller of the Currency could not represent a bank in a dispute with that agency if she had audited that bank's books while working for the agency. But she could represent the same bank (after a one-year cooling-off period) if her work at the agency had been to design general procedures for government auditors.

COOLING-OFF PERIOD. Former employees at level GS-17 or above are subject to a one-year ban on communications made with intent to influence their former agencies in any particular matter pending before that agency.[17] This restricts former government employees from lobbying their former agencies for one year after leaving government. It applies to all particular matters, even those in which the former employee was not personally involved. The ban applies only to communications intended to influence; it does not bar social contact.

There are some exceptions to the one-year ban. A former employee may communicate on matters on which he or she has "special knowledge" that is valuable to the agency or to furnish scientific or technical information. Former employees may respond to requests for information from their former agencies. Furthermore, former employees who go to work for state or local governments, Indian tribes, colleges, or hospitals are exempt from the one-year ban.

A former Internal Revenue Service employee, for example, cannot lobby the IRS on interpretations of tax-exempt status of church schools for one year after leaving, even if she had nothing to do with that decision while in government. But a former Office of Management and Budget employee could lobby the IRS on that topic because the IRS is not his former agency.

AREAS OF FORMER RESPONSIBILITY. The statutes prohibit former government employees, regardless of rank, from representing anyone on matters that were within the former employee's official responsibilities during the last year of his or her government service.[18] This two-year ban applies even to matters in which the former employee was not personally and substantially involved. For these purposes, "official responsibilities" are defined by statute, regulations, written delegation of authority, or job description.

For example, a former regional director of the Bureau of Alcohol, Tobacco, and Firearms (ATF) in Boston could not represent an indicted firearms smuggler within two years after leaving government if the smuggler's arrest had been made by ATF agents in the Boston office, even if the former employee did not work on the particular case. The former employee could represent that smuggler if he had worked in the Los Angeles office of the ATF because the matter would not have been within his official responsibility during his last year in government. Note, however, that the one-year cooling-off period would not permit such representation before ATF during the first post-employment year.

REPRESENTATION BY PERSONAL PRESENCE. On the theory that some highly visible former employees might influence a government decision by their mere presence on one side, a two-year ban on certain former senior employees prohibits their representation by personal presence in particular matters in which they participated personally and substantially.[19] This bars any personal appearance, even a silent appearance, before the government to assist in representing anyone in a matter in which the former employee was personally involved.

The former employee is not prohibited from assisting someone appearing before the government; the ban is on appearing with them. The Office of Government Ethics determines which former senior employees are covered by the ban, but it has been applied primarily to presidential appointees.

For example, a former IRS commissioner could not sit at the witness table beside a company president trying to get the Tax Court to uphold a ruling that the former commissioner had made while heading IRS, even if he said nothing during the hearing. The former commissioner could sit at the witness table if the case involved a ruling made by his predecessor before he entered government.

TRADE OR TREATY NEGOTIATIONS. The Ethics Reform Act of 1989 imposed a one-year ban on any former government employee using nonpublic information about trade or treaty negotiations in which the former employee personally and substantially participated to knowingly represent, aid, or advise any person other than the United States. This applies to all former employees, regardless of rank, but it applies only to matters in which the former employee participated personally and substantially.

ADVISING FOREIGN GOVERNMENTS. In response to wide publicity of a former Reagan administration official leaving government service and immediately becoming a lobbyist for foreign clients, a second post-employment restriction was added by the Ethics Reform Act of 1989. This is a one-year ban on any former officer or employee at GS-17 or above who represents, aids, or advises any foreign government with the intent to influence a decision of any officer or employee of the United States.

This very broad restriction is not limited to particular matters, to one's former agency, or to matters in which one participated personally and substantially.

Negotiating for Future Employment

The potential for conflict of interest is especially acute when a federal employee is planning to leave the government and begins to negotiate for future employment. Because federal policy provides for no severance or transition compensation for departing employees, most feel the need to begin a job search while still on the federal payroll. The danger occurs when they negotiate with future employers who are also federal contractors or otherwise engaged in a relationship with the government.

To prevent conflicts of interest under these circumstances, government-wide and agency-specific policies regulate the process of negotiation for future employment. The basic principle of these regulations is that government employees should consider a potential future employer, with whom negotiations for employment are under way or anticipated, as a source of conflict of interest, what is sometimes called a prohibited source.

Negotiations for future employment can begin before leaving government, unless the employee is a procurement officer in which case more stringent guidelines apply. Once negotiations for future employment occur or are anticipated, government employees must disqualify themselves from participation in any matters in which the future employer has a financial interest.[20] Many agencies also require their employees to notify the agency when they begin to negotiate for future employment.

For example, a Federal Communications Commission employee whose work involves analysis of long-distance phone rates could not negotiate for

future employment with AT&T without disqualifying himself from participation in any matter in which AT&T might have a financial interest. But
that same employee would face no restrictions on performance of her government duties if she were negotiating for a job in catalog sales with Land's
End, though perhaps she would be required to notify her agency that she
was discussing future employment with that company.

Appearance of Impropriety or Conflict of Interest

In 1965 President Lyndon B. Johnson issued Executive Order 11222, which
established what has come to be known as the appearance standard. It directs
federal employees to avoid any action, whether or not specifically prohibited,
which might result in, or create the appearance of, using public office for private gain, giving preferential treatment to any person, impeding government
efficiency or economy, losing complete independence or impartiality, making
a government decision outside of official channels, or affecting adversely the
confidence of the public in the integrity of the government.[21]

None of these general prohibitions is self-enforcing, and they are often
ambiguous in their application to specific situations. As a consequence, the
appearance standard itself has been vexing since its creation—to those who
must abide by it and to those who enforce it. Is it primarily aspirational and
does not have the full legal force of any other ethics regulation. Uncertainty
about enforcement has long prevailed. One former OGE director said, for
example, "Take a look at the language in the executive order: 'might result in
or create [the appearance of] an impropriety.' You can hang anybody on
that language. That's my problem with it. A guy who wants to screw you can
screw you. . . . It's not a good enough standard for me."[22]

Cures for Conflict of Interest

Many federal employees, especially among the ranks of presidential
appointees, have assets or other financial interests that pose a conflict of
interest. Most ethics regulations seek technical ways to cure those potential
conflicts, so that they do not prevent a person from entering or staying in
the federal service or from carrying out the full range of his or her official
duties. Complying with the ethics laws, says A. B. Culvahouse, who served as
counsel to President Ronald Reagan, "has really nothing to do with ethics or
morality as one might learn it in church. It's more like math."[23]

How does one avoid conflicts of interest that might result in self-dealing?
The process begins with consultation. For presidential appointees and some

other very senior government officials, the consultations usually involve the White House counsel's office, the Office of Government Ethics, and the DAEO at the agency where the appointee will serve. The individual's financial disclosure forms are reviewed and potential conflicts are identified. Then ethics officials and the individual discuss ways to cure the potential conflict.

This process developed in the first years after passage of the Ethics in Government Act of 1978. The act itself provides little guidance about how conflicts are to be resolved, and the early implementers of the act had to create procedures on their own. J. Jackson Walter, appointed by President Jimmy Carter to be the first director of OGE and then reappointed by President Reagan, described the purpose of these procedures.

> In a sense, OGE's advance review and clearance process amounts to prospective enforcement of criminal laws by requiring nominees to take precautionary steps to stay out of harm's way. . . . The tools and techniques available to fashion prospective cures generally are adequate to the task of bringing nominees into compliance with the conflict of interest laws. . . . In nearly all cases, it has been possible to design remedies that nominees and their families do accept. The costs associated with these remedies, particularly in terms of tax liabilities and disruptions of personal and family financial planning, in specific cases can be high. The conflict of interest statutes occasionally can be characterized, therefore, as a legislative limitation on presidential recruiting because they represent fundamental standards of eligibility for federal public office-holding with which not all the highly qualified persons in the country may choose to comply.[24]

President Reagan's first counsel, Fred F. Fielding, describes the process as it unfolded on the White House end in 1981:

> In this Administration—the first to undergo a full-scale Presidential transition under the 1978 Ethics Act—the virtually unvarying practice has been to have the financial disclosure report prepared and reviewed in draft form, both by the Counsel to the President and OGE, before a nomination goes forward and the final version of the form is formally filed and available to the Senate, press and public. This procedure helps insure that the final disclosure report will comply fully with the law, and also helps the White House and OGE focus ahead of time

on whatever special financial arrangements—e.g. divestiture, or creation of a "blind trust"—may be necessary in a given case. Also, it allows a hard look—the last one before the nomination and the candidate's private financial affairs become public—at whether the prospective nominee is financially and otherwise willing and able to make the adjustments the law requires as conditions to assuming the office.[25]

When a potential conflict is identified, several possible cures are available. In most cases, the option sought provides sufficient isolation of the individual from a conflict of interest with the least impact on the individual's personal finances.

Waivers

Waivers are often granted by ethics officials for situations in which the size of a personal financial holding is so small or the chance of a conflict so remote that it seems unnecessary to take any curative action. Such a waiver simply permits the official to conduct his responsibilities free from the need to dodge issues that might provoke concerns about a potential conflict of interest.

There are two statutory types of waivers.[26] The employee's agency may grant waivers on a case-by-case basis for financial holdings "not so substantial as to be deemed likely to affect the integrity of the services which the Government may expect from the particular employee." Or an agency may publish regulations in the *Federal Register* waiving a specific type of financial interest held by the agency's employees, if it is determined that the interest is "too remote or to inconsequential to affect the integrity of the Government officers' or employees' services." In addition, the 1989 ethics law authorized OGE to establish some governmentwide de minimis standards for waivers.

For example, a nominee to the Consumer Products Safety Commission (CPSC) may hold ten shares of stock in General Electric (GE), which his grandfather gave him as a college graduation gift decades earlier. GE does make consumer products, among many other things, and the CPSC does have regulatory authority over those consumer products manufactured by GE. But GE products are such a small portion of the responsibilities of the CPSC and the size of the holding is so small that no decision made by the agency could possibly enrich the nominee in any significant way. In such a case, a waiver might well be granted.

Disqualification

The least impact on personal finances is achieved when a satisfactory cure comes from disqualification. This requires no sale of assets. Instead, the individual agrees to recuse herself from any matter involving a stated company or organization in which she has a personal financial interest. Usually this is done with a signed recusal statement, but none is required by law.

Recusal statements are a common cure for potential conflicts of interest involving particular matters. They are especially useful when an individual has a financial asset that is only peripherally related to his government responsibilities, something that would only rarely—if ever—pose a potential conflict. Then the government employee can simply keep clear of the infrequent decision where that financial holding poses a conflict.

But recusal agreements are sometimes problematic. Personal financial holdings tend to change over time. A recusal agreement may not be permanently valid, particularly for those with complicated portfolios. And a recusal is not the appropriate cure in many cases in which the relationship between personal financial holdings and the core of a government employee's responsibilities is frequent and direct. In those cases, a recusal statement may prevent a federal official from effectively discharging the duties of office because potential conflicts occur frequently.

For example, a candidate for director of the Bureau of Land Management in the Interior Department might hold some stock in General Motors. Given that the director rarely makes decisions that directly affect General Motors, it would be reasonable to cure a potential conflict of interest through disqualification. The candidate would agree to participate in no decisions—procurement of agency vehicles, for example—in which his General Motors stock would pose a conflict of interest.

But if the candidate had stock in a large livestock holding company, many of whose subsidiaries lease grazing rights on federal land, a recusal statement is unlikely to be an effective or appropriate cure. So many of the bureau's policies deal with the use of federal lands that the director could not reasonably recuse from every one of those decisions to avoid a conflict of interest. Some other cure would be necessary.

Divestiture

When a potential conflict of interest looms too large to be cured by a recusal statement, the best option may be to sell, give away, or otherwise divest the asset.[27] In the eyes of the law, no financial conflict of interest can occur when an asset is no longer in the possession of the government official.

For example, a former executive of Boeing, coming into government as an assistant secretary of the Air Force, would have little recourse but to divest the $800,000 she owns in Boeing stock. Boeing is a principal supplier of aircraft to the Air Force, and no one could avoid constant conflicts of interest while performing the duties of a high-ranking Air Force official if she had significant holdings in Boeing. A recusal statement would not work as a cure in this case because it would impose too many constraints on the employee's performance. Divestiture, at least from the government's perspective, is a far more effective cure.

Divestiture is the most radical of the surgeries used to cure conflicts of interest. It is problematic in several ways. One is that it can be expensive, especially for presidential appointees just entering government service. If they have no choice but to divest certain assets, they also have no control over the market value of those assets at the time of the divestiture. The price of a stock, for example, might be substantially below the price at which it was acquired. Buying high and selling low is not a good investment strategy, but some presidential appointees find that following that strategy is the cost of entering public service.

The opposite situation can have problematic consequences as well. An asset may be substantially more valuable at the time divestiture is required than it was when acquired. In that case, the divestiture can have painful capital gains tax impacts. For many appointees coming into government service from lucrative jobs in the private sector, those unanticipated tax liabilities occur simultaneously with a significant drop in income—a double whammy.

A reform of the ethics regulations in 1989 lightened the burden of some of these forced divestitures by permitting government employees to seek a certificate of divestiture at the time an asset is sold. This is a formal declaration from an agency ethics official to the Office of Government Ethics that an asset was sold to avoid a conflict of interest and it permits the seller to defer tax liability while in government service.

Qualified Blind Trusts and Qualified Diversified Trusts

For the rare appointee who has significant wealth, including concentrations of stock in companies that would be harmed by the appointee's divestiture of that stock, another cure is available: the blind or diversified trust. The assistant secretary of the Air Force with Boeing stock would have a different situation if she were president of a company that did a significant amount of business with the Air Force and of which she was the founder and a principal stockholder. To divest her holdings would flood the market with her company's stock and, in all likelihood, drive down its price. This would have harmful consequences for the company's other stockholders and perhaps for the survival of the company itself. It might not even be possible to sell all of the stock, at least not at one time. In such circumstances, a blind trust may be the only realistic cure.

A qualified blind trust is one in which a government official places certain assets that are then managed by an independent trustee.[28] The trustee's fiduciary responsibility is to maximize the value of the trust's assets consistent with prudent financial management policies. But, importantly, the trustee must not report to the owner of the trust the specific transactions or the specific holdings of the trust. Nor may the trustee be encumbered in terms of what can be bought or sold in the trust. The trust is "blind" in the sense that the government employee is in the dark about the specific holdings that compose the trust. These are called qualified blind trusts because they have to be approved, or qualified, by the Office of Government Ethics, to provide an adequate cure for potential conflicts of interest.

A qualified diversified trust is composed of assets spread widely over a number of holdings with no more than 20 percent of the total in any one industrial, economic, or geographical sector and no more than 5 percent invested in any one issuer (other than the United States).[29] It, too, must be certified or qualified by the Office of Government Ethics.

The use of such trusts is uncommon because they are complex, they rarely provide an instant cure for potential conflicts of interest, and most people of financial means are reluctant to surrender oversight of their assets. They meet the needs of only a very small minority of government employees. At the end of 1997, only nineteen qualified blind trusts were in existence for the entire executive branch.[30]

The Enforcers

When ethics became an attractive, or perhaps necessary, political issue in the decades after 1961, Congress and the president began to construct the existing ethics edifice. But it was not enough simply to add new laws and rules, even thousands of pages of those in the law books. To ensure independent and vigorous enforcement of those ethics regulations, major institutional construction also occurred. Some of this was simple augmentation of existing agencies such as the FBI, the Justice Department, and the White House counsel's office. Some involved reorganization of existing functions, as with the replacement of the Civil Service Commission with an Office of Personnel Management and a Merit Systems Protection Board. But some of it, too, was original creation, especially the inspectors general, the independent counsels, and the Office of Government Ethics.

When the dust settled—if, in fact, it has settled—the ethics landscape was populated by a variety of agencies, each with a sizable piece of regulatory responsibility. The operative theory of those who engaged in this institutional construction project was that, with enough detectives on the force, no ethical slipup would go undetected or unpunished.

Federal Bureau of Investigation

The FBI has investigated crimes and potential crimes since its founding in 1908. Some of those involved violation of the criminal statutes regarding the behavior of public employees. But the FBI took on another role in ethics regulation in 1953 when President Dwight D. Eisenhower issued Executive Order 10450.

In the early days, the full-field investigations usually involved a couple of dozen field interviews with acquaintances, business associates, and neighbors of the nominee. The responses to the interviews were collected, and the file of raw information was passed on to the White House counsel for review. The executive order left it to department and agency heads to designate "any position within his department or agency the occupant of which could bring about, by virtue of the nature of the position, a material adverse effect on the national security as a sensitive position."[31] That Eisenhower's appointees, on average, were confirmed within eighty-nine days of his inauguration suggests that the full-field investigation was a relatively brief stop on a nominee's road to confirmation.

The overheated security passions of the early 1950s eventually began to fade, but the FBI full-field investigation never went away. It has remained in place to this day, and—like so much of the appointment process—it has grown steadily thicker and longer. By the late 1980s, the full-field investigation usually involved thirty-five or more field interviews, and the requirement was imposed on a vastly larger number of nominees than in 1953. A typical full-field investigation took twenty-five days to complete.[32] What had begun as a national security clearance had evolved into something much broader and deeper: a comprehensive exploration of every aspect of a nominee's character and background. Here is how the FBI now characterizes the topics it explores:

> Agents interview people who know the candidate, including references, associates, superiors, supervisors, colleagues, co-workers and neighbors. The principal areas to be addressed—commonly referred to in FBI terminology as CARL (A) B FAD—include character (C), a person's general attitude and possession of characteristics such as trustworthiness, reliability and discretion or lack thereof; associates (A), types of persons, groups, or organizations with which a person has been associated, with particular concern as to whether any of these associations have been of a disreputable or disloyal nature; reputation (R), the individual's general standing in the community; and loyalty (L), the person's attitude and allegiance toward the United States. Certain BIs also address the candidate's substantive ability (A) in the area of the prospective appointment, e.g., judicial appointees and persons affiliated with the Department of Justice. Ability is an individual's capacity or competence to perform well in an occupation or field of employment. Other areas addressed are bias/prejudice (B), an irrational attitude directed against any class of citizen or any religious, racial, gender, or ethnic group or their supposed characteristics; financial responsibility (F), lifestyle or spending habits consistent with the candidate's means; alcohol abuse (A), excessive use of alcohol impacting upon the candidate's behavior; and illegal drug use/prescription drug abuse (D), any use of illegal drugs or abuse of prescription drugs.[33]

Like many aspects of the appointment process, the FBI full-field investigation has expanded and changed in response to defining events. For example, when a Supreme Court nominee of Ronald Reagan was forced to withdraw after some of his former law students revealed that he had smoked marijuana with them, the FBI intensified its inquiries into drug use by the subjects of its investigations. Later, when former senator John Tower's nomination to be secretary of defense ran into heavy opposition in the Senate because of charges that he drank excessively and was alleged to be a womanizer, the FBI was embarrassed that its investigation had not adequately discovered or delved into those charges. The full-field investigations were enhanced to prevent future embarrassments.[34]

Over the years, the bells and whistles have accumulated so that now the full-field investigations are very wide-ranging and increasingly time-consuming. The FBI warned before the presidential transition of 2000 that the average investigation would take thirty-five days.[35] In reality, in 2000 the average FBI full-field investigation for candidates for presidential appointment took 44.4 days.[36]

Remarkably, in spite of their length and penetration, these investigations rarely produce information useful to the people who manage the presidential appointment process. What the FBI produces is a file of raw and unedited interview material. Little or no effort is made to verify or follow up on information that is critical of nominees. Much of it, therefore, is little more than uncorroborated hearsay.

What the FBI file does often do, however, is provide fodder for the opponents of a nomination. Since the initiation of full-field investigations, FBI files on nominees have been shared with the chair and the ranking minority member of the Senate committees with jurisdiction over the nomination. The file sometimes provides enough hints of scandal or misbehavior that an opponent can call for more investigation to delay action on a nominee or encourage interest groups to intensify their opposition. Those who wish to prevent a nominee from being confirmed could rarely improve on the raw data in the FBI file to cast doubt on the individual's character. In the confirmation controversy over John Tower's appointment to be secretary of defense in 1989 and in the battle over Anthony Lake's nomination to head the Central Intelligence Agency (CIA) in 1997, the FBI files of the candidates became the target of raiding parties by their political opponents.

"FBI raw files are raw files," Sen. Richard G. Lugar (R-Ind.) noted in response to the Lake confirmation battle. "They may be true, they may be false, they may be scandalously defamatory."[37] Even former FBI director William Webster notes that these files are "often freighted with hearsay, rumor, innuendo, and unsubstantiated allegation."[38] But FBI files are used more widely and are available to a larger number of senators now than ever before. The only logic that seems to be driving this expanded use of FBI files is a kind of perversion of the Golden Rule: Do unto them what they did unto us. The result is a constant expansion of the outer limits of acceptable senatorial conduct inspired by an escalating cycle of political paybacks.

Office of Government Ethics

OGE's institutional structure has changed several times since its creation. It began as a unit of the Office of Personnel Management. As a result of the Office of Government Ethics Reauthorization Act of 1988, it became a separate agency on October 1, 1989.

Since its creation as a product of the Ethics in Government Act of 1978, the Office of Government Ethics has taken the lead in ethics training and conflict prevention for federal employees. It also bears primary responsibility for periodically reviewing and recommending changes in ethics laws and regulations.

OGE works with the DAEOs to provide programs and published materials that help federal employees understand their ethical obligations and perform their duties within the boundaries established by the ethics regulations. OGE develops for congressional approval the financial disclosure forms used by all federal employees who are required to reveal their personal finances. It audits the forms submitted by presidential appointees and then works with them to identify and cure potential conflicts of interest.

OGE also keeps records of its decisions in individual cases and publishes a regularly updated set of opinion letters. These form the precedents that OGE, other agencies, or a federal employee may turn to in trying to determine a proper course of action in an ethically complicated situation. Opinion letters are often provided by OGE to employees seeking a safe harbor—competent and written ethical advice sought before they act and upon which they can later rely for protection if their behavior is questioned.

The current structure of the Office of Government Ethics is indicated in figure 4-1.

Counsel to the President

The president's attorney, the counsel to the president, has taken on a steadily expanding role in applying the ethics regulations to presidential appointees. This role is largely informal because the statutes say little about the White House counsel. But given that compliance with financial disclosure and conflict-of-interest requirements are largely legal and technical matters and because the staff of the Office of Presidential Personnel concentrates principally on recruiting presidential appointees and plays little role in facilitating their transition into new administration posts, ethics concerns have fallen by default to the counsel.

This role in the appointments process has imposed steady growth pressures on the counsel's staff. Lloyd Cutler, who served as counsel to Presidents Carter and Bill Clinton, noted that "in Carter's day when I came in, including myself, there were six lawyers. Twenty-five years later under Clinton, there are probably 40 lawyers, 50 lawyers. Part of that is dealing with the attacks on the President, and these enormous vetting responsibilities that descend on the White House Counsel."[39]

Figure 4-1. *U.S. Office of Government Ethics*

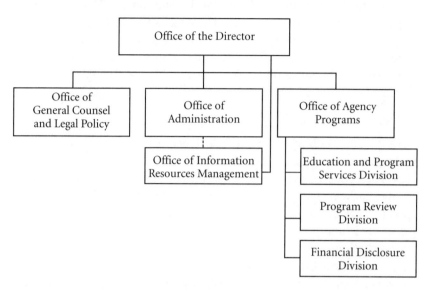

Source: Adapted from U.S. Office of Government Ethics, *Fifth Biennial Report to Congress* (Government Printing Office, April 1998), p. 7.

Once an individual has agreed to be the president's nominee for an appointed position, he or she meets with an attorney in the counsel's office for a discussion of the ethics regulations. During these meetings the candidate is given the forms and questionnaires that have to be completed as part of the process. They are numerous, detailed, and complex. The counsel's staff is often required to assist candidates in filling them out. Once completed, the forms are reviewed by the counsel's staff and the candidate is often interviewed again to follow up on potential problems. The financial disclosure forms then go to the Office of Government Ethics for the official audit. This may lead to further discussions in which the counsel's staff is involved.

The counsel is also the recipient of the findings of the candidate's FBI investigation. These, too, are reviewed and may lead to further discussions with the candidate. When the nomination is formally announced and sent to the Senate for confirmation, the counsel may have a continuing role as protector of the secrecy of the FBI file and as the president's representative in any discussions with the Senate involving ethics concerns about the nominee. C. Boyden Gray, counsel to George H. W. Bush, noted of the function:

How much of the FBI files do they get to see[?] We conduct the search; we do the FBI for our benefit not for their benefit. . . . That was subject to enormous negotiation. . . . Huge fights over that. . . . You have to negotiate them one by one. . . . Once you concede to one committee, you can't cut back for another committee; they're going to demand the same treatment. But it's got to be renegotiated and reinvented every time.[40]

Independent Counsels

In the aftermath of Watergate, reformers searched for a better way to investigate crimes alleged to have been committed by high government officials. Their concern resulted from the ancient problem of the foxes guarding the chicken coop. To them, Watergate highlighted the deficiencies of a system in which the leaders in an administration were investigated and prosecuted by Justice Department officials who were part of the same administration.

To remove what they viewed as the inherent conflict of interest in such circumstances, the reformers proposed a procedure in which an attorney general who believed sufficient evidence was available to require an investigation of a senior executive branch official could call for the appointment of an independent counsel to conduct the investigation.[41] This procedure was established by Title VI of the Ethics in Government Act of 1978.

Under the provisions of the act, the attorney general is required to conduct a preliminary investigation, lasting no more than ninety days, whenever he or she receives information that any federal criminal law has been violated by the president, vice president, cabinet-level official, senior White House aide, senior Justice Department appointee, director or deputy director of the CIA, Internal Revenue Service commissioner, national campaign manager, or campaign committee chair for the current administration or the previous administration if it was controlled by the same party as the current one.

If the attorney general finds evidence sufficient to warrant further investigation, he or she must then ask a special three-judge unit of the District of Columbia Circuit Court of Appeals to appoint an independent counsel. Once such an appointment is made, the independent counsel has the power to perform all investigative and prosecutorial functions of the Justice Department and cannot be removed before the completion of the investigation except in rare circumstances.

The initial independent counsel authority was limited to five years, but it was reauthorized by Congress in 1983 and 1988 for five years each. The authority lapsed on December 15, 1992, but was renewed in June 1994 at President Clinton's urging. When the independent counsel authority again expired in 1999, neither house of Congress passed renewal legislation.

The first independent counsel was appointed in November 1979 to investigate charges of illegal drug use by Hamilton Jordan, chief of staff to President Jimmy Carter. The last independent counsel appointed was in May 1998 to investigate charges of influence peddling by Labor Secretary Alexis Herman. Over the years between these dates, a total of twenty independent counsel investigations were conducted.

Public Integrity Section, Criminal Division, Justice Department

The Justice Department has always had primary jurisdiction for investigation and prosecution of corruption charges against federal officials involving potential violations of federal law. In 1976 Assistant Attorney General Dick Thornburgh established the Public Integrity Section as a component of the Justice Department's Criminal Division. The Public Integrity Section was assigned responsibility for overseeing federal anticorruption efforts at all levels of government and for prosecuting crimes related to elections. In so doing, the section works closely with U.S. attorneys and other prosecutors and investigators.

The section has primary responsibility for allegations of criminal misconduct that involve federal judges. Because U.S. attorneys must try cases before federal judges in their districts, the Department of Justice requires them to recuse themselves from any investigation involving those judges. The Public Integrity Section takes the lead on those cases. Since 1978, the section has had additional responsibility for supervising the independent counsel provisions of the Ethics in Government Act, during the times that provision was in effect.

From 1995 through 2000, the Public Integrity Section employed an average of twenty-nine full- and part-time attorneys. Its expenditures during that period averaged $5.2 million per year.[42] In the six-year period, the Public Integrity Section filed a total of 163 cases, approximately 28 a year on average.[43]

Inspectors General

The post-Watergate mentality yielded more in 1978 than just the Ethics in Government Act. It also produced the Inspector General Act of 1978. This was legislation intended to place independent and objective guardians of good government in each of the major federal departments. Subsequent amendments to the Inspector General Act increased the number of departments and agencies with statutory inspectors general to fifty-seven in 2000. The inspectors general now also operate two units that deal more broadly with ethics regulatory matters: the President's Council on Integrity and Efficiency (PCIE) and the Executive Council on Integrity and Efficiency (ECIE).

Specifically, the act created the position of inspector general (IG) and assigned to those officers responsibility for (1) conducting and supervising audits and investigations relating to the programs and operations of the relevant organization; (2) providing leadership and coordination in recommending policies for activities designed to promote economy, efficiency, and effectiveness in the administration of, and to prevent and detect fraud and abuse in, the programs and operations of the organization; and (3) providing a means for keeping the head of the establishment and Congress fully and currently informed about problems and deficiencies relating to the administration of such programs and operations and the necessity for and progress of corrective action.

Inspectors general are appointed by the president with the advice and consent of the Senate, and at the major departments and agencies they may be removed only by the president. They report to the head of the department or agency, or some other officer designated to receive such reports, but the appointed leaders of the organization may not prevent the IGs from initiating an investigation.

Other Enforcement Agencies

Other federal agencies have specific responsibilities for ethics regulation, even though those may not be the principal focus of their work. The Office of Personnel Management, for example, supervises the provisions of the Hatch Act that regulate the political activities of career employees. OPM also enforces portions of the Whistleblower Protection Act, ensures compliance with antinepotism rules in hiring, and superintends training programs that include ethics orientations.

The Merit Systems Protection Board protects the integrity of federal merit systems and the rights of career employees. It oversees federal personnel practices and conducts special studies of the merit system. The MSPB also hears and decides charges of wrongdoing and employee appeals of adverse agency actions—including violations of the Standards of Ethical Conduct.

The General Services Administration is responsible for the appropriate use and management of all federal property and equipment. It determines and enforces restrictions on improper employee use of frequent-flier benefits. And it enforces restrictions against gambling on government property and has some jurisdiction over gift regulations.

The Office of Management and Budget supervises the lobbying restrictions on recipients of federal contracts, grants, and loans. With the Office of Federal Procurement Policy, it manages the procurement integrity regulations.

The data in table 4-2 provide a fuller picture of the roles and responsibilities of all the agencies that participate in the regulation of executive branch ethics.

The Ethics Edifice

Washington, D.C., at the dawn of the twenty-first century, is an ethics supermarket. The law books overflow with descriptions of, restrictions upon, and penalties for every imaginable form of venality in the public service. Shops of rule writers, advisers, trainers, investigators, and prosecutors dot the city. Washington has long been called a company town, but the ethics industry has become a major subsidiary of the "the company."

As the astute Washington observer Norman Ornstein has noted:

Every time we have a scandal or a purported scandal, we add in new rules. . . . We just keep on adding them. We never streamline. We never rationalize. We never take away.

That we've kept doing this, but one could also argue that in the process of adding them in, you create not better ethics but more likelihood of violations of ethics and rules because you can't avoid violations, even if they're technical ones.[44]

It would not have been possible to imagine in 1961 how the ethics impetus would multiply, or how broad and diverse its yield would be. Piece by piece, the reformers have constructed the most detailed set of ethics regulations and the most extensive network of implementers ever to exist in any country in the history of the world. Those reformers found the magic formula—convince the market that more ethics regulation and more ethics regulators were the key to more government integrity—and they sold that

Table 4-2. *Ethics Regulatory Edifice for the Executive Branch, 2000*

Regulation	Responsible agencies
Standards of ethical conduct for employees of the executive branch; regulations on public and confidential financial disclosure, outside employment limitations, ethics training, certain financial interests, and post-government employment	Office of Government Ethics (OGE)
Conflict-of-interest statutes	OGE; Department of Justice (DOJ), Office of Legal Counsel
Hatch Act provisions; Whistleblower Protection Act; complaints of prohibited personnel practices	Office of Special Counsel; Office of Personnel Management (OPM) (certain Hatch Act regulations)
Criminal political contribution and activity restrictions	DOJ; individual U.S. attorneys offices
Appropriations law and contract protests; frequent flyer miles	Comptroller general, General Accounting Office (GAO); General Services Administration (GSA) (regulations on frequent flyer benefits)
Ethics audit reports	GAO; OGE
Prosecution of violations of criminal conflict-of-interest statutes	DOJ, including Public Integrity Section; individual U.S. attorneys' offices
Restrictions against gambling on government property, conduct "prejudicial to the Government"	OPM; GSA (restrictions on gambling on federal property)
General personnel and federal employment matters	OPM
Government Employees Training Act	OPM; OGE (ethics aspects)
Use of government-owned property and equipment, for example, phones, photocopying equipment	GSA; OGE (ethics aspects)
Official travel; use of government vehicles; gifts of travel from nonfederal sources	GSA; OGE (ehtics aspects)

Procurement integrity restrictions	Office of Management and Budget (OMB); Office of Federal Procurement Policy (OFPP); Federal Acquisition Regulatory Council (FARC); Department of Defense; GSA; National Aeronautics and Space Administration; OGE (ethics-related provisions)
Lobbying restrictions on recipients of federal contracts, grants, loans, and so on	OMB; clerk of the House of Representatives; secretary of the Senate
Restrictions against lobbying with appropriated funds	DOJ, Public Integrity Section
Appeals from disciplinary actions for violations of the standards of ethical conduct	Merit Systems Protection Board
Fraud, waste, mismanagement, and abuse in individual agencies	Agency inspectors general
Prosecutions of violations of the restrictions on outside earned income and outside employment for certain noncareer employees	DOJ, Civil Division; individual U.S. attorneys' offices
Prosecutions of failure to file or false filings of public financial disclosure reports	DOJ, Civil Division and Criminal Division; individual U.S. attorneys' offices
Nepotism	OPM
Gifts and decorations from foreign governments	Department of State, Office of Protocol; GSA (regulations on disposal and minimal value)
Coordination of governmental efforts to promote integrity and efficiency and to prevent fraud, waste, and abuse in federal programs	President's Council on Integrity and Efficiency (PCIE); Executive Council on Integrity and Efficiency (ECIE)

SOURCE: Adapted from U.S. Office of Government Ethics, "U.S. Government Entities with Ethics–Related Authority" (http://www.usoge.gov/pages/forms_pubs_otherdocs [January 6, 2002]).

formula with great success. No one effectively questioned their assumptions, and few attempted to review the impacts of their efforts.[45]

But the time is ripe for some stock taking. What has this vast expansion of ethics regulation, this tightened net, produced? And at what cost? Has government integrity improved significantly? Have the benefits of implementing this regulatory scheme justified its costs?

CHAPTER FIVE

To What Effect?

In few areas of public policy was there such durable momentum over the second half of the twentieth century as in the creation of new ethics regulations. The principal supporters of ethics regulation had several objectives in crafting these new regulations. They wanted to define public integrity—and its violations—with more clarity than ever before. They wanted to deter those violations. They wanted to identify violations when they occurred and punish the violators. And, as a result of all this, they wanted the American people to have greater faith and trust in their government.

The Big Question

Assessing the level of public integrity in America and comparing current levels with previous eras is no simple matter. No reliable historical measures exist of government integrity or government corruption. The terms themselves have so many meanings and are subject to such widely varying understandings that agreeing on a proper measure, let alone applying it over many decades, is probably impossible.

Scale poses a problem as well. Most of the new ethics regulations of recent decades have focused on what might be called "petty ethics," on the behavior of individual government employees in the day-to-day performance of their jobs. They should not steal government property, for example, nor act with bias in favoring one citizen over another, nor participate in decisions where they have personal financial interests. Law books are filled with comprehensive definitions of those kinds of ethical "Thou shalt not's." And a sophisticated bureaucratic machinery has been built to train, supervise, investigate, prosecute, and punish those who are subject to them. Right and wrong are clearly defined now, and the right is protected and the wrong prosecuted with more vigor than ever before on these matters of petty ethics.

But on the question of grand ethics the issues remain vexing, and the regulatory machinery is rarely of much help in resolving them. Should public officials lie, if they do so to serve important public purposes—protecting covert operations or maintaining secrecy about military planning, for example? Should American agents assassinate foreign leaders and terrorists if national security clearly benefits? Should Americans engage in torture if that is the only way to obtain information that might have enormous public benefit? Should regulators reveal investigations in progress if doing so might save shareholders and consumers from unnecessary risk but might also cause the value of a company's stock to drop before it is found guilty of anything illegal?

These morality questions go far beyond the more easily defined situational concerns of daily government operations. And even if the integrity of daily job performance by public employees were significantly improved, broad dissatisfaction may exist with a government in which officials lie or assassinate or torture. Or for that matter with a government that permits legal abortions, does not prevent the spread of pornography over the Internet, prohibits public prayer in schools, or tolerates executions of criminals.

Integrity and morality become fused and confused on these larger issues, and little of the ethics regulation momentum of recent decades has simplified or answered the questions they raise. So, in important ways, the best we can hope for—or, at least, we can hope to assess—is improvements in the integrity of public officials as they perform their routine duties. But how can even that be measured? How can we determine whether the mountain of new ethics regulations has raised government integrity to new heights?

The answer is that we cannot, not with any fine degree of precision, not with certainty. And comparing the public ethics of this era with that of past eras will be nearly impossible because not much is known about the daily performance of public duties by government officials of past eras. We only know what was reported by journalists and scholars who were far fewer in number than now, equipped with far fewer tools and resources than their contemporary counterparts, and reported to a public far less interested in a smaller and less salient federal government than the current one.

In the absence of perfect or precise tools of assessment, we have no choice but to work with surrogates. We must measure what we can measure, assess what we can reasonably assess, and compare our findings with what we know about earlier times. This may not tell us everything we would like to know about the impact of our current collection of ethics regulations, but it will tell us something. We must then try to make reasonable interpretations of what we find.

For example, we cannot determine with certainty that the public financial disclosure requirements deter bad people from entering government or permit public agencies and private overseers to detect every conflict of interest. But answers to questions about the process of making such disclosure divulge much. Who files these forms? How often are they examined and by whom? Does it seem likely that public financial disclosure serves the intended purpose of exposing government employees' personal finances to sufficient scrutiny to deter conflicts of interest and self-dealing?

Similarly, the full incidence of scandal and corruption in government cannot be measured. Presumably, some corruption goes undetected and its magnitude or severity remains unknown. But information about corruption can be obtained in some other ways, imperfect though they may be. For example, newspaper reports of real or alleged scandal can be tallied and studied to determine what they specifically say. Much of what the American people feel about integrity in government is based on these reports in the communications media. So the content of those reports is worthy of some analysis.

And we can look at the legal actions taken against those accused of corruption or ethics violations. Some data are available from before the passage of the Ethics in Government Act of 1978. While some corrupt acts are undetected and unprosecuted, and complete information cannot always be obtained, long-term trends in ethics law enforcement can be examined to see what can be learned from them.

Finally, there is the important question of public trust and confidence in government. Much of the new ethics regulation was aimed at elevating public trust and confidence, restoring what Watergate and other scandals had diminished. Perfect measures of this also do not exist. But public opinion polling is a bustling enterprise, and many surveys over the years tracked the trajectory of public trust and confidence. We also have other data on the engagement of citizens in government and their opinions of the integrity of those whom government employs. Surrogates though they may be, they are useful nevertheless for the insights they offer.

Deterrence

The theory of deterrence as it presently operates in the federal government holds that public officials are more likely to act with integrity when three conditions prevail. First, they must know and understand the general parameters of permissible behavior, the do's and don'ts of the ethics standards. Second, their personal finances must be examined by independent auditors and must be isolated from potential conflicts of interest. Third, they must be aware that their personal finances and their actions, and any connection between them, are subject to constant scrutiny.

The first of these conditions relies on training and education, which are the task of each agency and department, of the Office of Personnel Management, and especially of the Office of Government Ethics (OGE). Training and education are the foundations of any successful program of ethics regulation. This is especially true for officers at the top of the federal government, most of whom are presidential appointees and many of whom are new to public service and unfamiliar with its unique rules and standards.

Compliance with the second condition begins with an employee's annual completion of a personal financial disclosure statement. Lower-level employees file with their designated agency ethics official (DAEO); presidential appointees file with the Office of Government Ethics. In theory, the financial disclosure statements are then reviewed by the relevant ethics officials, and if potential conflicts of interest are identified, the employee takes action—recusal, divestiture, negotiation of a waiver, and so on—to cure the potential conflict.

The third condition is dependent on public access to personal financial disclosure reports. The assumption that guided the proponents of the Ethics in Government Act of 1978 to require public financial disclosure was this: Public officials would be inspired to avoid self-dealing if they knew anyone could view their financial disclosure statements and assess their public decisions in light of their personal finances. The proponents recognized that public disclosure would invade the personal privacy of thousands of federal employees. They also came to understand that completing the detailed financial disclosure forms was a vexing and time-consuming activity for many of those employees. They even understood that some talented private citizens would decline opportunities for public service because they wanted to protect their privacy. On balance, however, they believed that subjecting the personal finances of public officials to anyone's scrutiny was in the public interest.

While we now have more than two decades of experience with the financial disclosure requirements established in the Ethics in Government Act, it is not possible, retrospectively, to examine the full record since 1978. Under the law, agencies and OGE are required to retain personal financial disclosure forms (Standard Form 278, or SF-278) for only six years. The same is true of the forms filed by those who wish to view an employee's public disclosure form (OGE Form 201). Those requests are also retained for only six years.

So we were forced to limit our examination of the public use of SF-278s to 1995 and subsequent years. In early 2001, we requested from OGE all of the OGE-201s then on file. Later in 2001, we collected all of the OGE-201s that had been filed that year—most of them for new appointees of the George W. Bush administration. We analyzed and categorized those forms, noting the name of the person whose SF-278 was sought for viewing, the position that person held in the government, and the occupational category (journalist, researcher, attorney, and so on) of the filer of the OGE-201 who was seeking to view an employee's SF-278. We also interviewed a sizeable sample of agency DAEOs to determine their experience with the financial disclosure forms that are filed at their agencies and departments.

What we learned from these inquiries is that the overwhelming public response to the financial disclosures of senior federal officials is massive indifference. Most public disclosure forms in this period (99.3 percent) were never requested by anyone. They sat in file cabinets, undisturbed until six years passed and they were destroyed. In the six years from 1995 through 2000, there were only 1,003 requests to view the SF-278s of Senate-confirmed presidential appointees, 167 a year on average. These requests were for the SF-278s of only 405 federal officials, with most of the clustering around the public disclosure forms filed by cabinet secretaries and other cabinet-level officers. Only five appointees who did not meet with the president's cabinet had their SF-278 requested as many as ten times in this six-year period.

Further penetration of these data suggests that the totals are inflated by the work of one researcher, Professor Richard W. Waterman of the University of Kentucky, who had requested 105 SF-278s for ambassadorial appointees. We contacted Waterman, who indicated that his interest in the SF-278s was not related to questions of conflict of interest or other ethics matters. He was studying the "determinants of presidential choice of ambassadors."[1] When the requests generated by the Waterman study are subtracted from the totals, there was an average of only 150 OGE-201 filings each year.

Table 5-1 identifies the twenty appointees whose SF-278s were requested more than ten times in the six-year period. Figure 5-1 groups the requests into several categories of frequency. Only a handful (140) of those appointees' financial disclosure forms that were viewed at all were requested more than once. The single request was by far the modal experience among those SF-278s that were requested for viewing.

When we looked at requests to view financial disclosure forms by position, the findings were not surprising. The largest number of requests were for the disclosure forms of appointees of cabinet rank, even though these officials represent a very small portion of all filers. Figure 5-2 identifies the distribution of requests to view financial disclosure forms by executive branch position. The requests for ambassadorial disclosure forms were unusually inflated by a single researcher whose study of ambassadors was unrelated to ethics issues.

As of spring 2002, we were able to examine briefly the OGE-201 requests for 2001. The outset of a new administration brought an upsurge in requests to view the SF-278s of Bush appointees. There were 1,887 such requests in 2001 to view the SF-278s of 540 Senate-confirmed appointees (including some still on file from Clinton administration officials)—more requests than in the previous six years combined. Eleven hundred and fifty-four of those requests came from journalists. The bulk of the others came from the Democratic National Committee (318) and from labor unions (399).

In 2001, as in the previous six years, the vast majority of the requests clustered around a small number of top officials. The SF-278s of only fifty officials were requested more than five times. Sixty-four percent of the SF-278s examined were requested no more than twice, usually only by the Democratic National Committee or a labor union. Table 5-2 identifies the appointees whose SF-278s were requested more than ten times in 2001.

Financial disclosure is a highly useful component of any scheme of ethics regulation. It serves the educational purpose of reminding federal employees at least once a year to examine their personal finances and assure themselves and their agencies that none of what they own conflicts with what they do. The financial disclosure statement is essential as well for ethics auditors who work with employees to identify and cure potential conflicts of interest.

But neither of those important justifications for financial disclosure require public disclosure. Employees can be reminded of the relationship between their assets and their work without public disclosure. And ethics auditors can do their work without it as well. Both conditions are met each year for the more than 260,000 career employees whose personal financial disclosure forms are filed confidentially.

The protection of government integrity that is supposed to result from public disclosure may be achieved in some way by the mere act of public disclosure and the knowledge this imparts on the filer that his or her disclosure form might be viewed by someone sometime. This follows the dictum attributed to Dr. Johnson that nothing is so conducive to a good conscience as the suspicion one is being watched.[2]

But the chastening effect of public disclosure is quickly diminished when it is not accompanied by public scrutiny. For the vast majority of public filers, "the knowledge one is being watched" is entirely imaginary if it prevails at all. Most presidential appointees are not being watched by anyone outside of the government, certainly no more closely as public filers than they would be as confidential filers.

The three federal officials, none of them presidential appointees, whose public disclosure statements were sought most often between 1995 and 2000 were President Clinton (eighty-five requests), Vice President Al Gore (eighty-two requests), and Independent Counsel Kenneth W. Starr (eighty-seven requests). Yet these requests apparently were not significantly generated by any concern about conflicts of interest or self-dealing on the part of any of the three. Most of the press stories resulting from examinations of the financial disclosure forms were about their net worth and investment patterns.

The American public, even American journalists, have little interest in the bulk of the public disclosure statements of presidential appointees and other government officials. Most of the thousands of public disclosure forms filed every year are never viewed by anyone outside the government. Those few that are subjected to scrutiny rarely result in the detection of self-dealing or conflict of interest that has not previously been cured under the law. That is rarely the purpose of the scrutiny. In light of all this, it is hard to sustain the argument that public financial disclosure is essential to government integrity.

Table 5-1. *Executive Branch Employees Whose Financial Disclosure Form Was Viewed Ten or More Times, 1995–2000*

Name	Position	Number of requests	1995	1996	1997	1998	1999	2000
Robert E. Rubin	Secretary of the Treasury	38	11	3	10	7	5	2
Alexis Herman	Secretary of Labor	36	4	2	22	6	1	1
Alan Greenspan	Chair, Federal Reserve Board	18	2	3	8		3	2
John M. Deutch	Director, CIA	17	10	3	1		2	1
Ronald H. Brown	Secretary of Commerce	16	14		2			
William M. Daley	Secretary of Commerce	16			8	4	1	3
Madeline K. Albright	United Nations (UN) representative; Secretary of State	14	1	1	7	3	2	
Bruce Babbitt	Secretary of the Interior	14	5	2	3	3		1
Andrew M. Cuomo	Secretary of Housing and Urban Development	13	1	4	7	1		
Henry Cisneros	Secretary of Housing and Urban Development	12	8	1		3		
Federico Peña	Secretary of Energy	12	6	3	2	1		
Janet Reno	Attorney General	12	3		3	4	1	1
Lawrence Summers	Secretary of the Treasury	12	1	1	3	1	5	1
William S. Cohen	Secretary of Defense	11			5	3	3	
Arthur Levitt	Chair, Securities and Exchange Commission	11	1	3	1		3	3
William J. Perry	Secretary of Defense	11	6	4			1	
Franklin D. Raines	Director, Office of Management and Budget	11		2	8	1		
Richard C. Holbrooke	UN representative	10			5	5		
William E. Kennard	Chair, Federal Communications Commission	10	1		4	1	1	3
Charles O. Rossotti	Commissioner, Internal Revenue Service	10			1	3	3	3

Source: Analysis of Office of Government Ethics Form 201.

Figure 5-1. *Frequency Distribution of Requests to View Appointees'*
Financial Disclosure Forms, 1995–2000

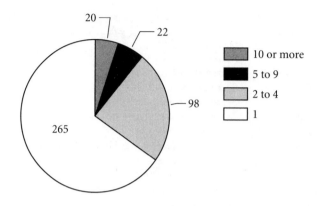

Source: Analysis of Office of Government Ethics Form 201.

Figure 5-2. *Distribution of Requests to View Financial Disclosure Forms,*
by Position, 1995–2000

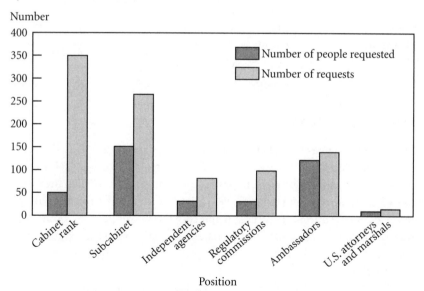

Source: Analysis of Office of Government Ethics Form 201.

Table 5-2. *Executive Branch Employees Whose Financial Disclosure Form Was Viewed Ten or More Times, 2001*

Name	Position	Number of requests
Colin L. Powell	Secretary of State	55
Paul H. O'Neill	Secretary of the Treasury	51
Donald H. Rumsfeld	Secretary of Defense	49
Donald L. Evans	Secretary of Commerce	43
Gale A. Norton	Secretary of the Interior	41
Christine Todd Whitman	Administrator, Environmental Protection Agency	41
Tommy G. Thompson	Secretary of Health and Human Services	38
Spencer Abraham	Secretary of Energy	35
Ann M. Veneman	Secretary of Agriculture	35
John Ashcroft	Attorney General	33
Elaine L. Chao	Secretary of Labor	33
Norman Y. Mineta	Secretary of Commerce	33
Roderick R. Paige	Secretary of Education	29
Melquiades Martinez	Secretary of Housing and Urban Development	28
Mitchell E. Daniels Jr.	Director, Office of Management and Budget	28
Anthony J. Principi	Secretary of Veterans Affairs	25
Robert B. Zoellick	U.S. trade representative	20
Harvey Pitt	Chair, Securities and Exchange Commission	19
Joe M. Allbaugh	Director, Federal Emergency Management Administration	14
Michael Powell	Chair, Federal Communications Commission	13
Paul Wolfowitz	Deputy Secretary of Defense	12

Source: Analysis of Office of Government Ethics Form 201.

Frequency of Scandals

In the study of government ethics, few challenges are more vexing than trying to measure the frequency with which corruption or scandal occurs. Formal investigations by government agencies are rare, relative to the number of government employees, even to the number of presidential appointees. Prosecutions are rarer still and convictions rarest of all. If one uses the measure of legal violations pursued through the justice system and proven in court as the measure of corruption in government, there is very little to describe.

Why then is there so much public discussion and debate about government corruption and the flawed ethics of public officials? Part of the answer is that there is no common definition of corruption and the term is widely used in the press and in public discourse to describe any allegation however faint and fleeting, however inaccurate, of questionable judgment or disagreeable consequences in the actions of public officials.

Much of this is in the eye of the beholder. When a member of a regulatory commission seeks to verify factual charges with a company under investigation by seeking information from the company, for example, that may seem like prudent procedure to members of the employee's political party. To political adversaries, however, it may seem like improper consultation. If no formal accusation is made against the commission member or investigated and resolved by official agencies, there is no reliable test of whether corruption or even bad judgment occurred. But the action and the accusations are likely to make it into press reports and add to the accumulation of stories that generate public perceptions of government corruption.

Another factor in these perceptions is the pattern common to stories of government corruption. They have legs. Stories in which substance is thin can go on for weeks or months at a time. That they produce few real indicators of improper action and no official charges, indictments, convictions, or sanctions may matter little to the life of the story so long as the subject is a visible public figure and an audience is interested. The news and the law are driven by different imperatives.

Professor Larry J. Sabato explained the character of such stories in his book *Feeding Frenzy*:

> As the frenzy takes hold, the press becomes mesmerized by the subject and obsessed with the target. "The press absolutely blocks out every other topic and can't talk about anything else," says Ellen Hume, formerly of the Wall Street Journal. Journalists get carried away, caught up in an overreaction of their own making. With a loss of perspective, they cease making judgments about how much is too much and instead lock into the story line for the duration of the unfolding soap opera.[3]

Adding to the attention paid to stories of government corruption is an important dynamic of modern politics. Ethics is a battleground of contemporary partisanship. When one party fails to beat the other in an election or fails to gain control of Congress, it often turns to other tactics to prevent the winners from governing freely. One of those tactics is questioning—even castigating—the ethics of opposition officials. When one party controls

Congress and its principal investigating committees, and the other controls the White House and staffs the administration—the common pattern in American politics for the last half century—the opportunities for politically inspired and politically charged ethics investigations are constant and inviting.

The operative theory here seems to be that an administration will find it harder to implement policies distasteful to its opponents if the implementing officials are distracted, diminished, or destroyed by criticisms of their integrity. Investigations have become one of the principal weapons of modern political warfare, and few handles serve this purpose more effectively than the array of ethics regulations that may now be used as standards of judgment against incumbent federal officials. As political scientists Benjamin Ginsberg and Martin Shefter concluded in their book *Politics by Other Means,*

> The issue of government ethics and the growing use of criminal sanctions against public officials have been closely linked to struggles for political power in the United States. In the aftermath of Watergate, institutions such as the Office of the Independent Counsel were established and processes to investigate allegations of unethical conflict on the part of public figures were created. Since then political forces have increasingly sought to make use of these mechanisms to discredit their opponents. . . . The creation of these investigative processes, more than changes in the public's tolerance for government misconduct, explains why public officials are increasingly being charged with ethical and criminal violations.[4]

So we are left with an incommodious dichotomy. Worry about the ethics of public officials greatly exceeds formal evidence of ethical violations. How then do we assess or measure the frequency with which ethics standards are violated and the severity of those violations? Consistent and reliable indicators simply do not exist.

One surrogate, though hardly a scientific one, is to examine newspaper coverage of federal employee ethics. We conducted a comprehensive examination of newspaper and magazine articles focusing on the ethics of federal officials in the forty years from the beginning of the Kennedy administration to the end of the Clinton administration. We used the normal indexes of such articles and searched for those whose titles included keywords such as "ethics," "scandal," "corruption," and so on.[5] We defined our coverage

broadly and with few constraints. If an article indicated that a federal official had misbehaved, even if it only reported allegations of such misbehavior, we reviewed and coded the article. We made no effort to impose a nar-
row or legal definition of ethics or corruption. We were principally
interested in what a typical citizen might think about the frequency of corruption or scandal in government from regular and attentive reading of the
major newspapers.

We learned several things. First, journalists and their editors apply few
consistent standards in describing ethical violations or reporting corruption. Unverified allegations, spurious charges, political attacks all make
news. Furthermore, the resolution of these charges and accusations rarely
receives coverage equal to the lodging of them. In the Reagan years, many
more stories were published, for example, about charges against Labor
Secretary Ray Donovan, his federal indictment, and his resignation than
about his subsequent acquittal. James Beggs, National Aeronautics and
Space Administration head under Reagan, received more coverage for his
indictment and resignation than for the subsequent decision of the Justice
Department to drop all charges against him. President Clinton's first agri-
culture secretary, Mike Espy, was indicted on thirty criminal counts, many
of them involving violations of gift rules and other ethics regulations.
Charges against him were the subject of frequent news coverage for years—
much more coverage than attended his acquittal on all charges.

This is the typical pattern. Stories about alleged ethics violations have
long legs. They appear for months, even years, as charges are alleged, investigated, and prosecuted (or not). The resolution is usually a much shorter
story, especially if it is an acquittal or dropping of charges or decision not to
indict. The subject of the story endures months of negative publicity and a
tarnished reputation. If vindication does finally come, it is rarely loud
enough or long enough to erase the damage. "The acquittal," writes Larry
Sabato about scandal coverage in the news media, "never catches up with
the allegation."[6]

We also learned that the number of actual crimes or even serious ethics
violations reported in these stories is relatively small compared with the
total number of stories—and stratospherically rare compared with the
total number of federal officials. We found 299 separate executive branch
employees who were the subjects of stories about corruption, scandal, or
ethical improprieties in the years and newspapers we examined. From this
list we eliminated 186 stories that dealt with people under consideration
for jobs or nominated for jobs but never confirmed, family members of

Table 5-3. *Individuals Subject to Newspaper Stories about Alleged Ethical Violations or Improprieties, by Administration, 1961–2000*

Administration	Number of individuals
John F. Kennedy	4
Lyndon B. Johnson	9
Richard M. Nixon	2
Gerald R. Ford	5
Jimmy Carter	9
Ronald Reagan	48
George H. W. Bush	18
Bill Clinton	18
Total	113

Source: Analysis of standard indexes of periodical articles.

executive branch employees, or offenses so inconsequential or unproven that they failed to meet even a broad definition of public corruption. For example, we eliminated a story about a federal employee alleged to have shoplifted $5.66 worth of groceries from a convenience store in Virginia and another about an employee who had accused his staff of using "communistic" language and of having been "trained in Moscow." We also limited our attention to stories about the ethics concerns that are the focus of ethics regulations: bribery, self-dealing, supplementation of salary, conflict of interest, and so on. Our totals then did not include many allegations relating to Watergate, Iran-contra, or Whitewater. Breaking and entering, covering up campaign contributions, running a covert foreign policy, and savings and loan irregularities are beyond the scope of ethics regulatory policies.

Table 5-3 summarizes the stories remaining after these refinements of the list. The unit of analysis is not the number of stories, but the number of people who were subjects of such stories. Some were the subjects of many stories.

We then followed up on each of these stories to determine whether it led to prosecution for the offense described. We had hoped also to include forced resignations as evidence of sanctions for improper behavior, but we found no way to reliably distinguish forced resignations from those that normally occur when political appointees leave government. Figure 5-3

Figure 5-3. *Prosecutorial Actions on Subjects of Ethics Stories, 1961–2000*

Number of stories

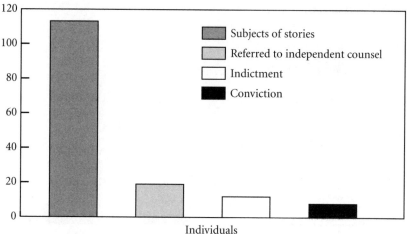

Source: Analysis of standard indexes of periodical articles and follow-up analysis of independent counsel data.

indicates the prosecutorial activities that resulted from the cases reported in these stories.

We were able to explore in more detail a case study of press coverage of ethics violations in the Reagan administration because of the existence of a study published in 1987 by the House Post Office and Civil Service Committee's Subcommittee on Civil Service. The subcommittee staff compiled newspaper and magazine articles, up to that date, that charged Reagan administration officials with ethics violations. This was an effort by a subcommittee controlled by Democrats to demonstrate the poor ethical record of the Reagan administration. We reviewed all of those articles and categorized each as either "serious" (potential rules violations), "questionable" (unlikely to involve rules violations), or "minor" (unrelated to ethics rules). Figure 5-4 summarizes our findings.

More smoke than fire? So it would seem. Press stories about corruption or ethics violations in the federal executive branch are often about innuendoes, unverified and never-proven charges, pregovernment imperfections, political potshots, and the kinds of minor oversights that are neither very surprising nor very criminal in the lives of busy leaders.

Figure 5-4. *Categorization of Periodical Reports on Ethics Violations in the Reagan Administration, 1987*

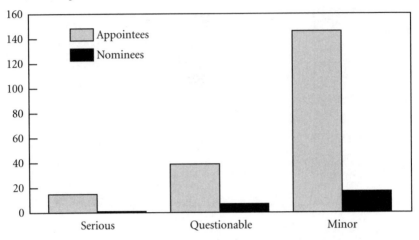

Number of reports

Source: Analysis of data from a fact book prepared by the staff of the House Post Office and Civil Service Committee, Subcommittee on Civil Service, in 1987. Republished as *All Four Feet and a Snout in the Trough: 200 Alleged Ethics Violations by Reagan Administration Appointees* (Diane Publishing Company, 1987).

These stories may contribute to a public perception that there is always some corruption going on in Washington, D.C. They may provoke and energize efforts to add new regulatory protections against corruption. They keep the fires stoked. But when one looks beyond the headlines, there simply is not much there.

Prosecutions and Convictions

The most important weapons in the war on scandal are the criminal statutes against such things as bribery, supplementation of salary, false and willful financial disclosure, and so on. One important measure, then, of the level of corruption in the executive branch should be the incidence of prosecutions and convictions under these statutes. The more often they are invoked, the more often they yield detection and punishment of criminal violation of standards of ethical conduct, the more powerful and persuasive the evidence of Washington's ethics problems.

One could also argue that criminal statutes serve an important deterrent function even if they are rarely used. Integrity flourishes, the argument would hold, when potential violators know the high price they would pay for breaching the public trust. Criminal statutes keep them in line and out of trouble.

Deterrent effects are impossible to measure because no one can identify foregone corruption or venality. But in other parts of the criminal justice system, deterrence rarely measures up to the hopes of those who write the criminal laws. More drug laws have not resulted in less drug-related crime. Wider use of capital punishment has not significantly reduced homicide rates where it is the ultimate sanction. The criminal law expands constantly, but so, too, does the jail population. Those who argue that a principal benefit of criminal sanctions for ethics violations is their deterrent effect will have a hard time proving their case, at least by analogy.[7]

So it is important to look at the pattern of prosecutions under these laws as clearer evidence of their impact on government integrity. Frequent prosecutions would suggest that ethical violations are common. A changing pattern of prosecutions—a steady increase, for example—would indicate that ethical violations are occurring more frequently or being investigated and prosecuted more aggressively. In a federal executive branch with more than two and a half million employees, the frequency of prosecutions of ethics violations should be some measure of contemporary levels of government integrity.

To explore this question, we collected evidence on prosecutions, indictments, and convictions of government employees at all levels from the annual reports of the Public Integrity Section of the Criminal Division of the federal Department of Justice. The Public Integrity Section was created in 1976 to oversee all prosecutions of ethics-related crimes in government. Its annual reports are the principal source of information about those crimes that entered the criminal justice system. Figure 5-5 indicates the pattern in indictments and convictions from 1970 to 1999. These are data on all federal officials, not simply the employees of the executive branch who have been the principal focus of this study.

The data are notable in several ways. First, they suggest some growth over time in the number of federal officials prosecuted for public corruption. From 9 in 1970 to 480 in 1999, one's initial impression is that there is more government corruption than there used to be.

But that is a misleading conclusion. One notes a dramatic increase in prosecutorial activity in 1983 and then a pattern that continues at the higher

Figure 5-5. *Indictments and Convictions of Federal Officials, 1970–99*

Number

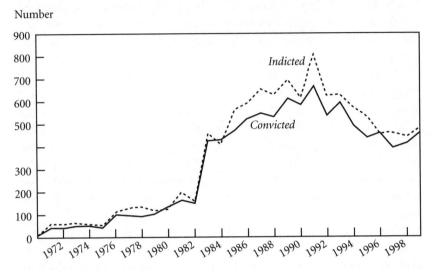

Source: U.S. Department of Justice, *Sourcebook of Criminal Justice Statistics 2000* (Government Printing Office, 2000), p. 482.

level thereafter. It is the sort of jarring alteration in pattern that always catches a social scientist's eye. We inquired into this change and found that it most likely reflects neither a change in the incidence of corruption or in the prosecution of it, but in the way crimes were reported. In 1983 the Public Integrity Section gave new guidance to U.S. attorneys' offices in reporting public corruption. Specifically, the guidance stated:

> For purposes of this questionnaire, a public corruption case includes any case involving abuse of office by a public employee. We are not excluding low-level employees or minor crimes, but rather focusing on the job-relatedness of the offense and whether the offense involves abuse of the public trust placed in the employee.[8]

So, much of the significant increase reported in 1983 and thereafter reflects a change in the definition of public corruption for reporting purposes, not a change in the incidence of corruption nor in the zeal or effectiveness of prosecution.

Another factor in the measurement of prosecuted public corruption is changing resources. Presumably the frequency and success of public corruption prosecutions is impacted by changes in the number of people assigned to investigate and prosecute public corruption. All prosecutors have to make choices: which cases to investigate, which to prosecute, which to take to trial, which to negotiate a plea bargain for, and so on. A primary element in those choices is limited resources. But as resources expand, so, too, do the opportunities to investigate and prosecute crimes that might have been overlooked or not pursued in the past when resources were more scarce.

Vast increases in the resources applied to the pursuit of public corruption are evident between 1970 and 1999. The statutory establishment of the offices of inspector general in many departments and agencies created a new force of officials one of whose principal tasks is to investigate and report corruption and violations of public trust. Inspectors general do not prosecute cases, but when their investigations suggest the commission of a crime, they are passed on to prosecutors in the Justice Department or the U.S. attorneys' offices. A study by Paul C. Light of the offices of inspector general in twelve departments and six major agencies identified a total of 3,503 employees in those offices in 1983 and 4,216 in 1990.[9] In 2000 the annual report of the Executive Council on Integrity and Efficiency indicated that all inspectors general in the federal government employed 11,000 people.[10]

Similar growth has occurred in the U.S. attorneys' offices. According to Suzanne Garment's study of government scandals,

[The U.S. attorneys], nearly a hundred of them, enjoy substantial freedom from Washington's control. In the past 25 years, their staffs have grown rapidly. In 1963 there were 657 lawyers serving as assistant U.S. attorneys. By 1980 there were 1,695 of these prosecutors, and the number in 1990 was around 3,000.[11]

In 2000 the National Association of Assistant United States Attorneys reported that the number of assistant U.S. attorneys had grown to 4,800, more than a sevenfold increase since 1963.[12]

The FBI also played a growing role during this period in the investigation of political corruption. The number of FBI agents grew from 7,600 in 1970 to 11,646 in 1999, and more of them were assigned to political corruption cases than ever before.[13] As political scientists Robert N. Roberts and Marion T. Doss Jr. conclude from their study of corruption investigations:

> In the years following Watergate, the Federal Bureau of Investigation made public corruption investigations a high priority. The FBI gathered evidence in almost every public corruption case brought before the Public Integrity Section or U.S. attorneys. By the early 1980s, the FBI moved from collecting evidence to setting up elaborate stings to test the honesty of public officials. The use of stings marked a major escalation of the federal war against public corruption.[14]

Add to all this the enactment in these same years of the independent counsel statute that created even more investigatory and prosecutorial resources aimed at detecting and sanctioning public corruption. The twenty independent counsel investigations between 1979 and 2000 spent nearly $200 million in this pursuit.[15]

The apparent increases in prosecutions for public corruption result from more than changes in reporting terminology and substantial growth in investigatory and prosecutorial resources. They result as well from the growth in ethics regulations and criminal statutes. If there is more lawbreaking, one of the explanations is that there is more law to break. The decades following 1961 produced a steady accumulation of new laws and regulations and new sanctions for those who violated them. As one Defense Department official noted to Suzanne Garment:

> There was a proliferation of rules and no one really understood them. I used to keep a copy of the procurement rules on my desk. Now I'd have to begin stacking them down on the floor to keep them even with the desktop. I don't think [the change took place] because the people involved are more evil. . . . But the job is getting increasingly complex. We're being asked to do harder things.[16]

The new laws and regulations also produced new sets of reporting requirements and cures for potential conflicts of interest. Each of these has become a potential source of new violations and prosecutions. The public financial disclosure requirements of the Ethics in Government Act of 1978, for example, are accompanied by significant penalties for inaccurate reporting that is "knowing and willful." These are designed to be prophylactic, to be an instrument of protection that prevents conflicts of interest.

But the reporting requirements themselves become a legal obligation with their own criminal sanctions. And since their establishment, charges of inaccurate or incomplete reports, though rarely criminal, have become yet another contribution to the public perception that government integrity is in decline—not because conflicts of interest occurred but because public employees erred in completing the reports designed to detect conflicts of interest. The scandal is not public corruption, but the failure to fill out the forms designed to prevent public corruption. It is a logic worthy of Alice in Wonderland.

So it is not remarkable in view of all this—more laws and rules, more investigators and prosecutors, more public and news interest in government scandals, and expanding definitions of public corruption—that measures of public corruption have inclined upward. What is remarkable is that the incline has been so gradual and the absolute number so low. Even with thousands of investigators and prosecutors available to pounce on evidence of government corruption, inspired by platoons of reporters ready to glorify their efforts to protect public integrity, the average annual number of convictions in the 1990s was only 503 in a federal executive branch that averaged more than 2.7 million full-time civilian employees in those years. At a time when more than 20 million crimes are committed in America each year, when more than 10 million arrests occur annually, when more than 1.3 million people are in state and federal prisons, any objective analysis would have to conclude that the federal executive branch is one of America's most reliable crime-free zones.

Public Confidence and Trust

Nothing was more important to the proponents of the Ethics in Government Act of 1978 than restoring and enhancing public trust in government. The successive shocks of Vietnam, Watergate, and several congressional scandals of the 1970s had knocked public trust to worrisomely low levels. It was widely believed that new fortifications for public integrity were essential to any effort to reverse the decline.

The steady accumulation of ethics regulations and the expansion in the strength and scope of enforcement were all justified in significant part by the need to raise public faith and confidence in the federal government. Many state and local governments followed suit for similar reasons. America's governments sought to clean up their act to regain the trust of America's people.

It is reasonable to ask if they succeeded. Do the American people have more confidence in the integrity of government than they did before the onslaught of new ethics regulations and enforcers?

There is no perfectly reliable way to know what the American people think on any topic at any moment. But some surrogate measures can help discern public opinion and, in this case, public confidence and trust in government.

One of those is public opinion as measured through opinion surveys. To determine whether changes have occurred over time in public confidence and trust, one would need surveys taken at many points over the past four decades or more. Because we began this research project in 1999, we had no way to do retrospective polling and have had to rely on polls done previously by other organizations for other purposes. We have carefully scoured the public opinion archives and discovered a variety of surveys that examine some of the issues that concern us. None of these asks the questions in just the way we would, had we been designing this research forty years ago. But there are enough surveys, close enough to the topic, to give us some sense of how public trust and confidence in government have changed over the years.

The most valuable of these surveys are those conducted every two years by the Survey Research Center at the University of Michigan as part of the American National Election Studies (ANES). To most political scientists, these are the gold standard of public opinion polling, carefully designed and tested, and administered consistently since 1958. While none of the ANES questions asks specifically about public evaluations of the performance of officials in the federal executive branch, our primary focus here, the ANES has consistently calculated an index of trust in government based on responses to several related questions. The greater the percentage, the higher the level of public trust. Figure 5-6 indicates the pattern of responses over time.

Opinion surveys also reveal that perceptions of the motives, behavior, and integrity of public officials play a critical role in public evaluations of government performance. A study by the Pew Research Center for People and the Press in 1997 (see box 5-1), for example, found that perceptions of public officials were the largest component of popular distrust of government.

Public confidence in government is measured in ways other than public opinion surveys. People express their trust with what they do and what they support as well as in what they say. The last four decades have produced a variety of indicators suggesting that the American people find few

Figure 5-6. *Trust in Federal Government, 1964–2000*

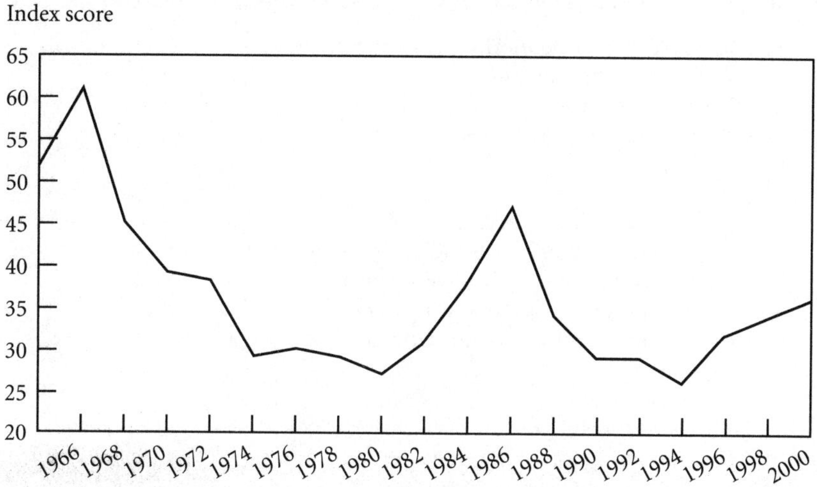

Index score

Source: Calculated from American National Election Study Trust in Government Index data (www.umich.edu/~nes/nesguide/toptable/tab5a_5.htm [January 15, 2002]).

reasons for faith or trust in their government. Our analytical tools are too blunt for the surgery necessary to determine how much of this behavior is a direct response to ethics-related concerns. But at the time the federal government has taken its most comprehensive and aggressive efforts to restore public faith in its own integrity, the American people seem not to have been persuaded.

This period of supercharged ethics regulation has coincided with one of the steadiest declines in electoral participation ever recorded, as the data in figure 5-7 indicate. The nearly half of eligible Americans who chose not to vote in presidential elections, and the even larger percentages who stay home during other elections, include many who are expressing a loss of faith in government.

Another indicator of diminishing trust in government officials is declining attachments to political parties. Parties have been the principal structural element of American politics since the beginning of the nineteenth century. Yet the past few decades have seen a growing distance between citizens and parties across the political spectrum. To many Americans, parties seem to represent a kind of politics—a kind of craven and dishonest politics—from which they wish to disassociate.[17]

Box 5-1. *Reasons People Give for Distrust of Government, 1997*

Political leadership or political system (40 percent)
    Politicians are dishonest or crooks
    Only out for themselves or personal gain
    Representatives say one thing and do another
    Too partisan
    Scandals
Critiques of government (24 percent)
    Too much government spending or spend money frivolously
    Federal government cannot get anything done
    Government is too big, too much government
    Government interferes too much, too intrusive
Policy (15 percent)
    Taxes are too high
    Dislike government policies, dislike specific policy
    Spend too much on foreign countries
    Government has the wrong priorities
Government does not care, is unresponsive (13 percent)
    Government does not pay attention to or care about people
    Needs and opinions of people not represented in government

Source: Adapted from Pew Research Center for the People and the Press, "Deconstructing Distrust: How Americans View Government" (http://206.65.84.148/trusttab.htm).

Much of this same distaste for traditional politics is seen in the willingness of Americans to support third-party candidates (such as Texas billionaire H. Ross Perot in 1992 and consumer advocate Ralph Nader in 2000) and to elect individuals to Congress who have never before held elected office (such as Sens. Jon Corzine, D-N.J.; Susan Collins, R-Maine; Paul Wellstone, D-Minn.; and John McCain, R-Ariz.). Recent decades have been a time when the best politics was antipolitics, when advantage flowed to those who suffered none of the perceived taint of having held public office or been at the center of public debates. Political virginity is persuasive evidence of purity to many voters, and thus an appealing antidote to the impurities they find in government.

There has been no clearer example of this than the term limits movement that thrived in the last decade of the twentieth century. This was a movement built on the simple notion that the accumulation of experience in public office was inevitably corrupting and that the only cure for it was

Figure 5-7. *Voter Turnout in Elections for President and House of Representatives, 1920–96*

Percentage voting

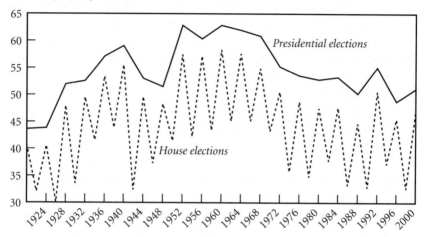

Source: Constructed from U.S. Census Bureau data.

forced removal. When scholars and other opinion leaders tried to present evidence to the contrary and indicated the high costs of term limits, the American people turned a deaf ear. When leading politicians, such as House Speaker Thomas S. Foley, D-Wash., took stands against term limits, they often put their careers in jeopardy.

In 1996 a Gallup Poll found that 74 percent of the American people favored a constitutional amendment imposing term limits on members of Congress. In 1999, 73 percent backed such an amendment.[18] Rational arguments against term limits were of little avail against a powerful public perception that government is corrupting and that too few politicians can resist its temptations.

The story told by the public opinion surveys and the recent behavior of American citizens is starkly relevant to the question about the relationship between ethics regulation and trust in government. From their high levels in the early 1960s, nearly every measure of trust in government steadily declined into the 1990s.[19] Through all the years when the federal government was adding more ethics regulations and more enforcers of those regulations, the American people either did not notice or were not persuaded that any of that was a justification for them to place more trust in their government.

The fortifications that the ethics regulators built did little to attract the confidence of the people they were designed to please most directly.

Or perhaps there was another dynamic at work. More ethics regulations and more ethics enforcers have produced more ethics investigations and prosecutions—not just legal investigations and judicial prosecutions, but congressional and media investigations as well. Whatever the new ethics regulations may have accomplished in cleaning up government, they have done little to reduce publicity and public controversy about the ethical behavior of public officials.

In fact, they have usually done the opposite. The more ethics regulations designed and implemented, the more personnel assigned to enforce them, the more the air has filled with news—often caustic and depressing news—about government ethics. The American people, though often ignorant of the details, have choked on the foul smell. The real state of public integrity is thus less important in determining levels of public confidence than the magnitude of news headlines that pierce public attention. Where there is smoke, most seem to assume, there must be fire. And, with more laws to violate, more personnel to investigate, more journalists to report, and more news outlets to publicize those reports, there has never been more smoke than in the past few decades.

So, not surprisingly, the expansion of ethics regulations and enforcement agencies and personnel has not produced a concomitant increase in public confidence in government integrity. The federal government today may be less corrupt than it has ever been, but that seems largely irrelevant to public confidence. The public has no way to know or measure the true level of integrity in government. It only knows what it hears and sees and reads. And all of those receptors are filled almost constantly with stories that, far from suggesting high levels of public integrity, too often suggest just the opposite.

Conclusions

The evolution of federal ethics regulatory policy over the last four decades of the twentieth century was inspired by a syllogism that went something like this: Public faith in the integrity of government is essential in a democracy to ensure public support for the policies of government. Integrity can be enhanced by clear and vigorously enforced rules regulating the behavior of government employees. The more of those rules there are and the more they guide and constrain the actions and decisions of public employees, the higher will be the level of government integrity and the greater will be public support for government.

So the federal government proceeded to enact a steadily accumulating body of ethics regulations followed by even more rapidly accumulating interpretations of those. It created new agencies to enforce these regulations and steadily beefed up the ethics enforcement capabilities of old agencies. It gave the public and journalists more and more information about the private lives of public officials so that the latter would always feel the hot breath of public scrutiny on their necks.

Did all of this activity produce higher levels of integrity in government? It probably did. But the conclusion has to be softened by several considerations.

No compelling evidence indicates that levels of government integrity were substantially lower before the flood of new ethics regulations began than they are now. No reliable or compelling evidence is available, for example, that employees of the Kennedy or Johnson administration were less honest or less devoted to the public interest than those of more recent administrations. Both administrations were largely scandal-free, at least by the standards and regulations of their time. The problem that the new ethics regulations were intended to address may have been exaggerated in the shadow of Watergate and a few other notable but largely aberrative scandals of the 1970s. The barn door has been closed and nailed shut on horses that had no intention of leaving.

The change in standards is another part of the problem of comparative assessments. Much behavior that occurred legally and openly in earlier generations would be offensive now. But it gave little offense then. Accepted practices evolve over time. Can we say that government was more corrupt at a time when what we now regard as corruption was not so regarded?

There is the further problem of changes in levels of publicity. Americans never know how much corruption is occurring in government. They only know how much is reported. In theory, levels of integrity could stay consistent over time while public perceptions declined because corruption was more often reported. It is entirely possible—in our view it is, in fact, the case—that employees of the federal executive branch operate today with as much integrity, as much devotion to the public interest, as they ever have. But there are more news outlets and reporters, and more competition among them, than ever before. One wonders how the integrity of the Coolidge or Hoover administrations would have been assessed if they had unfolded in an era of all-day, all-news television and radio, hidden cameras and microphones, the Internet, Matt Drudge, and hours of *Dateline*, *20/20*, and *60 Minutes* to fill each week.

The point here is that it is very difficult to establish an empirical connection between ethics levels and ethics regulation. If government integrity is high, as we believe it is, there is no sure way to explain that. Have all these regulations and the looming threat of so many investigatory and prosecutorial resources changed the incentives and behavior of government officials, turning crooks into clerics? Or are government employees, like most Americans, diligent, honest workers trying to perform their tasks efficiently and lawfully—and requiring no rigid codes and menacing overseers to force them to act that way? We suspect the latter comes closer to the truth than the former.

But even if one is willing to accept the premises inherent in the syllogism that new regulations and new enforcers have raised the level of government integrity in some significant way, this only begs another set of questions. At what costs have these benefits been obtained? And do the benefits justify the costs?

CHAPTER SIX

Contemplating
the Costs

Even if the accumulation of new ethics regulations over the past four decades was shown to have resulted in substantial improvements in the level of government integrity, a policy analysis would be incomplete without an assessment of the costs of accomplishing that. Making such an assessment requires answers to numerous questions: What is the cost in money and personnel to manage national ethics policy? What have been the costs of regulations imposed upon the target groups of the current ethics policy: presidential appointees and career civil servants? Have new ethics regulations made it more difficult to recruit private citizens to fill top government executive jobs than in the past? What impact does the ethics policy have on the efficiency of the presidential appointments process? Are presidents able to put their administrations in place in a timely fashion and are executive vacancies quickly filled? What impact has ethics policy had on relations between the executive and the legislature, on relations between Democrats and Republicans, on the government's ability to determine and serve the will of the American people? Have the new ethics regulations contributed to better government performance in Washington, D.C.?

Paying for Ethics: Budget Impacts

As new ethics regulations have been created over recent decades, new agencies have been established to implement and enforce them. Some existing agencies have also taken on larger responsibilities for ethics policy implementation and they have grown for that purpose. All of this growth incurs costs. It is not simple to measure those costs because some of the agencies that perform ethics functions have other functions as well, and their budgets do not clearly track the divisions of responsibilities or the dollars attached to each.

The Office of Government Ethics (OGE), for example, has a budget that is entirely devoted to activities related to ethics policy. The FBI, meanwhile, has some ethics-related responsibilities—investigating corruption and performing background checks on government employees—but it has many other duties that are not related to ethics policy. The portion of the FBI's annual outlays devoted to ethics functions is difficult to determine with accuracy.

While noting these difficulties, we have attempted to measure the budget costs of managing federal ethics policy. Table 6-1 has the outlays made by each of the relevant agencies in fiscal year 2000. Some of these agencies have many responsibilities other than ethics enforcement, but data were not available for ethics functions only. We were also unable to develop reasonable estimates for the costs of the Office of Counsel to the President and the designated agency ethics officials (DAEOs). All play key roles in ethics enforcement, but their separate budgets and personnel numbers are buried in much larger totals. The information in table 6-1, therefore, is only a rough indicator of the personnel size and dollar costs of the ethics edifice.

One important item not included in table 6-1 is the cost of independent counsel investigations. Independent counsel authority was allowed to expire in 1999, so there are no current expenditures for independent counsel investigations. But independent counsels played a highly visible role in ethics enforcement in the last two decades of the twentieth century, and an assessment of their cost is entirely relevant to this analysis. Though fewer than half of them yielded indictments, those investigations cost more than $207 million. Table 6-2 provides a summary.

Initiation Rites

Some of the most significant costs of federal ethics policy are borne by the individuals whose behavior this policy seeks to regulate: federal employees. For purposes of this analysis, it is useful to divide federal employees into two groups, presidential appointees and career civil servants, because ethics policy has a different impact on each.

Table 6-1. *Budget Outlays of Agencies on Ethics Policy Functions, Fiscal Year 2000*

Agency	Outlays (dollars)	Personnel
Office of Government Ethics	9,000,000	72
Offices of Inspectors General	1,300,000,000	11,000
Office of Personnel Management	211,000,000	3554
Merit Systems Protection Board	29,000,000	310[a]
Office of Special Counsel	10,000,000	106
Public Integrity Section, Department of Justice	5,617,000	31

Source: For outlays, *Budget of the United States Government, FY 2002*. Personnel data are from the websites of the relevant agencies or from telephone conversations with their human resources offices. The commitment of money and personnel by the FBI is also substantial, but estimated totals for either are not available.

a. Data for fiscal year 1999.

More than 280,000 employees of the federal government are required to make annual disclosure of their personal finances. On average, between 1995 and 2000, 262,138 of them were required to file confidentially. They complete the confidential personal financial disclosure form (OGE-450) and submit it to the DAEO in their agency for review by May 15 of each year.

The Office of Government Ethics estimates that the average time it takes to complete OGE-450 is one and a half hours. Using that estimate as a guide, we calculate that the number of hours spent across the federal government each year performing the responsibility for confidential financial disclosure is 393,207, or the equivalent of a full work-year for 191 people.

Other federal employees, approximately twenty-one thousand in number, are required to make public financial disclosure, using Standard Form 278 (SF-278). The Office of Management and Budget (OMB) estimates that it takes them an average of three hours to complete their annual financial disclosure requirement.[1] That totals to 63,000 hours, or 7,875 workdays per year.

Presidential and other political appointees, once in office, must file an updated SF-278 each year like the high-ranking career employees. But political appointees also have to endure other burdens when they enter the government. Financial disclosure is only one of those.

Perhaps the best way to describe the requirements faced by new appointees is to follow the process that an appointment typically follows before the selected individual can officially begin his or her duties. For most appointees, the process begins before they are contacted. The Office of Presidential Personnel in the White House is aware of a vacancy and begins

Table 6-2. *Summary of Independent Counsel Investigations, 1979–2000*

Independent counsel(s)	Date appointed	Subject of investigation	Results	Cost of investigation (dollars)
Arthur Christy	November 29, 1979	Hamilton Jordan	No indictment	215,621
Gerald Gallinghouse	September 9, 1980	Timothy Kraft	No indictment	3,300
Leon Silverman	December 29, 1981	Raymond Donovan	No indictment	326,000
Jabob Stein	April 2, 1984	Edwin Meese III	No indictment	312,000
James McKay Alexia Morrison	April 23, 1986 May 29, 1986	Theodore Olson	No indictment	2,141,000
Whitney N. Seymour	May 29, 1986	Michael K. Deaver	One guilty plea	1,552,000
Lawrence Walsh	December 19, 1986	Iran-contra affair	Seven guilty pleas, four convictions (two overturned on appeal), six presidential pardons	48,490,000
Carl Rauh James R. Harper	December 19, 1986 August 17, 1987	Lawrence Wallace	No indictment	50,000
James C. McKay	July 18, 1988	Lyn Nofziger Edwin Meese III	One convicted (overturned on appeal)	2,796,000
Name under seal	May 31, 1989	Name(s) under seal	Under seal	15,000
Arlin Adams Larry Thompson	March 1, 1990 July 3, 1995	Department of Housing and Urban Development	Seven guilty pleas, eleven convictions	29,255,982

Name under seal		Name(s) under seal		
	April 19, 1991	Name(s) under seal	Under seal	93,000
Joseph diGenova	December 14, 1991	Janet Mullins	No indictment	3,458,205
Michael F. Zeldin	January 11, 1996	Margaret Tutwiler		
Robert B. Fiske Jr.	January 24, 1994	Whitewater	Fourteen guilty pleas and convictions,	63,754,022
Kenneth W. Starr	August 4, 1994		impeachment of the president	
Robert Ray	October 18, 1999		(acquitted)	
Donald C. Smaltz and others	September 9, 1994	Mike Espy and others	Fourteen guilty pleas and convictions	24,212,582
David Barrett	May 24, 1995	Henry G. Cisneros	One guilty plea (pardoned)	15,624,720
Daniel Pearson	July 6, 1995	Ronald H. Brown	No indictment	3,626,914
Curtis Von Kann	November 27, 1996	Eli Segal	No indictment	516,534
Carol Elder Bruce	March 19, 1998	Bruce Babbitt	No indictment	6,289,064
Ralph I. Lancaster Jr.	May 26, 1998	Alexis Herman	No indictment	5,035,479
Total costs				$207,767,423

Source: "Revision of Special Prosecutor Law Cleared," 1982 Congressional Quarterly Almanac (Washington: Congressional Quarterly, 1983), p. 388; General Accounting Office, Financial Audits of Expenditures by Independent Counsels, GAO/AIMD-97-24R, GAO/AIMD-97-64, GAO/AIMD-97-164, GAO/98-100, GAO/AIMD-00-120, GAO/AIMD-99-292, GAO/AIMD-99-105, GAO/AIMD-98-285, GAO/AIMD-99-105, GAO/AIMD-99-292, GAO/AIMD-00-120, GAO/AIMD-00-310, GAO-01-505, GAO-01-1035 (Government Printing Office, various years).

Note: Figures are not final because some independent counsel investigations were ongoing at the time independent counsel authority expired.

a search for an appropriate candidate. This can be short and simple, as when someone high in the pecking order of power pushes a favored candidate for a particular post. But that is unusual. Far more typically, a search involves careful review of many candidates, some pushed into prominence by powerful political forces, others favored by interest groups, and some by members of the White House staff. In the mix as well will be candidates discovered by the personnel office through standard procedures of executive search. From this long list will come a short list, usually of three to six candidates, who are more carefully examined by staff.

The winnowing usually yields a single candidate who then becomes the focus of attention. The candidate is contacted to determine his or her interest in the job. If the response is positive, a long process of scrutiny and investigation begins. Part of this is political, aimed at determining whether the candidate is likely to be a loyal supporter of the president's program and whether he or she has accumulated any political enemies who might become a burden for the administration. There is a careful vetting among acquaintances of the candidate to get answers to these and other questions about suitability for the job.

But a major part of the investigations and clearances that occur in the prenomination stage involves compliance with conflict-of-interest and other ethics laws. Once a single candidate has been designated for the vacant position, the Office of the Counsel to the President gets involved.[2] A member of the counsel's staff will meet with the candidate and hand over a packet of materials that includes:

—The White House's "Personal Data Statement" questionnaire, a confidential, twenty-three-question document that usually must be filled out within twenty-four hours.[3] The questions run the gamut from medical condition to whether a candidate ever used illegal drugs after the age of eighteen, hired a nanny, joined a controversial group, wrote an article, or did anything that could embarrass "you, your family or the President."

—The U.S. Office of Personnel Management's Standard Form 86, "Questionnaire for National Security Positions." This form is needed for a security clearance and is a springboard for the FBI's full-field background investigation. It generally is not made public, but it will be forwarded later to the Senate. Some Senate committees may publish some or all of the answers with the hearing record, which is a public document. Among other things, SF-86 asks where the candidate lived, worked, and went to school; about all foreign trips taken; and whether the candidate ever consulted a mental health professional, had a criminal record, used controlled substances illegally, received treatment for alcohol abuse, or filed for bankruptcy. The White House asks candidates to fill out SF-86 within two weeks.

—The Office of Government Ethics' Standard Form 278, "Public Financial Disclosure Report" for executive branch personnel, which requires an exhaustive listing of all assets, liabilities, jobs, and board memberships. This form can be made public in its entirety upon request.

—A consent form for the FBI background investigation.

—A separate form allowing a check of the candidate's credit record.

—An authorization for release of medical information.

—A "tax check waiver" allowing the IRS to check the candidate's tax returns for the previous three years and tell the White House whether taxes were paid on time.

—The candidate is fingerprinted.

A Pentagon official said of this process, "The forms are unbelievable and they're redundant and annoying. They ask the same question three different ways to see if they can catch you. And then you go through this with three different organizations."[4]

Political scientist Terry Sullivan made a comprehensive study of the questionnaires and forms imposed on candidates for presidential appointments. He found that they required candidates to answer more than two hundred questions. He concluded, "The government cannot justify the burdensome repetitiveness of this process. The elaborate systems of inquiry needlessly confuse the nominees and represent an unnecessary burden on those so willing to serve."[5]

This is just the paperwork. Once the forms are completed, White House lawyers begin to review them. The staff of the counsel's office examines SF-278 then sends it to the DAEO of the relevant agency or department with a copy to OGE. These three offices will then consult as necessary to determine whether there are conflicts of interest indicated by the disclosure forms and what can be done to cure them. In most cases, once these negotiations are complete, the candidate will sign an ethics agreement that indicates the steps to be taken to come into compliance with ethics regulations. For many candidates for appointment, "coming into compliance" with ethics regulations usually requires a change in or surrender of control over parts of their financial portfolio, agreements to resign from organizations and boards of directors, or the execution of statements disqualifying them from participation in certain decisions. This signed agreement is usually part of the paperwork that accompanies the nomination when it goes to the Senate.

While this process is under way, the FBI full-field investigation begins. These investigations are conducted by the Special Inquiry and General Background Investigations Unit of the FBI. They are scheduled to be completed in thirty-five days, but they often take longer, especially at the beginning of a new administration when many appointments are in the pipeline. In 2000, for example, the average full-field investigation took 44.4 days to complete.[6] The full-field investigation is composed of several elements. One is a verification of the information provided by the candidate for the appointment: prior addresses, employment, military service, degrees earned, and so on. Another is a series of interviews, often several dozen, with people familiar with the candidate. These seek information about the candidate's reputation, character, use of drugs or alcohol, business practices, possible bias or prejudice, and financial responsibility.

The FBI collects the information from these interviews and sends it, without summary judgment, to the White House counsel's office. The FBI makes little effort to verify the comments received from the people it interviews. Its role is to collect comments, not to assess their validity. The candidate's FBI file is reviewed by the counsel's staff and is subsequently made available to the chair and ranking minority member of the Senate committee with jurisdiction.[7]

The FBI full-field investigation is discomfiting to many candidates for appointment. Those who are interviewed by FBI agents are told only that the subject of their inquiry is being considered for an unidentified position in the government. So the investigation becomes a sweep for information that might disqualify or harm the candidate's nomination. Especially troublesome is the raw information that remains in the FBI file. If one of those interviewed says something damaging to the candidate's character or reputation, that information is not verified and remains in the file. Even many of those who review these FBI files find the process distasteful and often not very useful.

When a Senate committee in 1977 looked closely at the value of these FBI investigations, it found little. One presidential personnel assistant called them a "disjointed, irrelevant collection of gossip." A former White House counsel said that he spent his first year at the White House reading the FBI files and found them full of "nonsense," "very poor jobs, second rate efforts." A personnel aide said they were "like Fibber McGee's closet—stuff just tumbles out."[8] In dozens of subsequent conversations with staff from the White House personnel and counsel's office, we have rarely heard an opinion different from this. "I'm at the point that I'm not sure the FBI check is absolutely necessary," said former health and human services secretary Donna Shalala. "They don't find anything for 99 percent of the people."[9]

Once all the information from the financial disclosure and ethics compliance review, tax check, criminal records check, and FBI investigation have been collected, the nomination is ready to go to the Senate. In a typical case, several months have already passed since the candidate was first informed that he or she had been selected or was under consideration for a position. During this time, said Louis Caldera, who served as secretary of the Army during the Clinton administration, "You're in limbo. You can't go ask people for business. You can't develop new business in good conscience when in fact you're thinking about leaving. So your whole life is in limbo; your kid's life is in limbo, your wife's life is in limbo."[10]

And then the limbo continues as the Senate takes over. In the last quarter of the twentieth century, the Senate confirmation process became more formalized, rigid, politicized, and elongated than it had ever been before. Senate committees have their own questionnaires and conduct their own investigations of nominees. Individual senators often investigate on their own and pick political fights with nominees over specific issues that play well in the senator's home state or may be a matter of personal pique involving the nominee or someone else in the administration. Sometimes ethics questions are used as stalking horses for this kind of delay and investigation. It may be that the real reason for opposition to a nomination is a policy difference between the nominee and one or more senators or between the administration and some Senate members. But senators are often reluctant to oppose a nomination solely on policy grounds, on the theory that a president is entitled to staff an administration with people who share the president's views.

But an ethics question often serves as a convenient handle for opposition when the real issue is policy. Democrats who disliked John Tower's views on defense policy or who felt they had been mistreated by him when he served in the Senate used questions about his integrity and probity to justify their opposition to his appointment as defense secretary in 1989. Linda Chavez's improper use of a household employee gave ample opportunities to her adversaries in the labor union movement to attack her nomination as secretary of labor in 2001 on ethical rather than policy grounds.

For those who wish to oppose a nomination in the Senate, the accumulation of ethics rules over the past half century is an enormous boon. Before there were fat FBI files full of raw data, before there were detailed listings of personal finances, before there were answers to lengthy questionnaires, it was simply much harder to find the soft underbelly of a nomination, real or imagined, than it is now. The information that nominees are required to provide as a routine part of the appointment process and the investigations undertaken as part of that process provide the best resources a political opponent could ever desire. It is not surprising that a growing number of nominations have been defeated or withdrawn over what appeared to be ethics concerns when, in fact, the real source of opposition was policy disagreement. Ethics is a far less slippery handle for an opponent than policy in a political system that subscribes to the belief that presidents are entitled to subordinates that share their views.

William B. Gould IV, a Stanford University law professor who was nominated by President Bill Clinton to chair the National Labor Relations Board, was a victim of this tactic in 1993 and 1994. During the nine months his nomination loitered before the Senate, those opposed to his views on labor law repeatedly sought an ethics handle for opposing his nomination, accusing him—without any factual basis—of running up large gambling debts in Las Vegas and of being connected to the Communist Party in Cuba and South Africa. Though his FBI full-field investigation had long since been completed, the allegations caused the FBI to go back into the field and to conduct an extensive interview with Gould himself.[11]

It is not hard to imagine the emotional burdens imposed on appointees forced to submit to a process that thoroughly explores their personal finances and every aspect of their lives; asks acquaintances to comment on intimate, personal questions; looks into appointees' medical, marital, and psychiatric histories; and then exposes them to public scrutiny through press leaks and plants as well as a public confirmation hearing in the Senate. Supreme Court Justice Clarence Thomas is famous for describing his ordeal as a "public lynching," but many other appointees have had similar bruising experiences. William Gould called the process "a complete roller-coaster."[12] "Something like a prolonged root canal without anesthesia," former CIA director Robert M. Gates called his passage through the process.[13]

Jocelyn Elders who served as President Clinton's first surgeon general said of her travel through the appointment process, "I felt it was more a mechanism to try to destroy me than anything else. I came to Washington, D.C., like prime steak and after being here awhile, I feel like poor grade hamburger."[14] Anthony Lake in 1997 withdrew his nomination to head the CIA after months of "search until you find something" investigation by the Senate Intelligence Committee that found little but delayed a vote. Lake said he had come to believe the committee would "nibble him to death rather than deal with the nomination straight-up anytime soon."[15]

The addition of so many new ethics regulations and requirements has contributed significantly to the lengthening of the appointment process and the invasive exposure and opportunities for embarrassment or opposition it imposes on nominees. There is no dollar value on these costs, but the experience and testimony of many of those who have endured these new burdens attests to the high personal costs they often inflict.

Turndowns

During the congressional debate on the Ethics in Government Act, opponents repeatedly warned that one of its primary impacts would be to keep good people from entering government. Even those who were honest, whose reputations were spotless, would not want to endure the months in limbo the ethics reviews and background checks would require, would not want themselves or their families subjected to invasive scrutiny of what they regarded as personal matters, and would not want to be part of a process they would regard as demeaning.

What impact has the ethics act had on presidential recruiting? The evidence here can never meet the standards of those who want to know "How many people have turned down administration jobs because of the Ethics in Government Act?" A person who is invited to join an administration faces a complex decision involving many different factors. And even if it were possible to count those who have been asked and have declined because of ethics requirements—and the data on that are more anecdotal than statistical—that would not provide a fully reliable answer. Some people make it clear before they are asked that they would not accept. Others offer one explanation for their turndown when, in fact, the cause is something else.

Fred Fielding, who served as counsel to President Ronald Reagan, had a clear vantage point on that administration's personnel recruiting efforts. He explained the difficulties in assessing the impact:

> The reasons that you're never going to have any real empirical studies and statistical review of the deterrent effect on recruitment . . . is that you don't know at which stage the people bow out. They can bow out when they first hear about the vacancy. They can bow out when they're talking to a political friend of theirs or a Senator or somebody

that they want to support them, and they suddenly hear about the [ethics requirements]. They can bow out when they're in the board room and say, "I'm going to take a run for it," and the guy next to them says, "Don't do it. They'll kill you." They can bow out when they're talking to the most junior-level personnel recruiter. You just can't keep statistics on this.[16]

Reports from the Front

In the absence of consistent data on the percentage of those invited to join an administration who decline to do so and the reasons they cite for declining, other indicators must be checked. One of those is the testimony of people who have served as counsels to the president and as directors of presidential personnel, the two senior White House positions with the most intimate involvement in the recruiting process.

White House personnel officers are never comfortable discussing recruiting problems. They see such problems as a reflection on the president and on their own persuasive powers—a negative reflection if the turndown rate is high. So, at least while they are in office, most paint a rosy picture of the president's success in attracting good people to serve in his administration. Later, however, after they have left office, a more realistic picture emerges.

Fred Malek, who served as personnel director for Richard M. Nixon in the early 1970s and then remained at the periphery of government in Washington in the years that followed, noted in 1984,

> I think overall our batting average was pretty high. I think today the pendulum has shifted a great deal. I think that there's a great preponderance of qualified Americans who really don't want to consider serving because of the "guilty until proven innocent" attitude that seems to prevail in the press and on the Hill. They've seen what so many people have gone through and so many people have had their souls bared. They just don't want to subject themselves to that. It's an intrusion on their privacy. It's an infringement on their reputation. It can affect their families and the way their kids feel about themselves and get treated at school. I think this kind of post-Watergate atmosphere has probably gone a little bit too far to the extreme and has really impacted on people's willingness to expose themselves to all that. They will make the sacrifice. They'll make the financial sacrifice. They'll move to Washington, but they're not going to put themselves through all that.[17]

E. Pendleton James, who worked in the personnel office during the Nixon administration and then served as director of presidential personnel in the first two years of the Reagan administration, found that the Ethics in Government Act, which had come into being in the interim, was the principal difference between the recruiting environments in those two periods. Of the act, he said, "It's horrendous, it's mind boggling, it's intimidating, and it inhibits attracting good people to government." He cited one prospect for an administration job who told him, "Pen, my financial disclosure document runs 32 pages. I don't think I've ever done anything dishonest in my life or made any shady deals, but the more I think about it, I don't want every staff member and member of the media going through my 32 pages line by line."[18]

James had earlier written,

A disappointing number of outstanding candidates for high government positions decline to serve. Facing the reasons for these turn-downs and doing something about them is urgently needed. . . . Government cannot offer its managers the financial rewards of the private sector, nor can it promise officials much privacy. But the laws, at least, ought not punish those who, with the best motives, are eager for public service. The public deserves to be served by the nation's best talent, and when the law deflects that talent, it is clearly not serving the public interest.[19]

John L. Moore, who served as a special counsel on conflicts of interest to the Carter-Mondale transition and later as president of the Export-Import Bank, worked during the Carter administration with a number of potential appointees. He found that the public disclosure requirements of the ethics act often discouraged their interest in serving. "I think the overall atmosphere has become awfully demeaning," he said, "and I think it's time that we spoke up for ways to adjust that problem. It may be more important in deterring people concerning government service than some of the technical aspects."[20]

R. James Woolsey, who served as undersecretary of the Navy during the Carter administration and as general counsel to the Senate Armed Services Committee, worried as well about the recruiting impacts of the public disclosure requirements. "I think the public disclosure element of the statute has been pushed too far," he said, "and it is one of the deterrents to getting people in, particularly those outside Washington from the business community, into Government. . . . It is, I think, a major deterrent to people outside government who are concerned about the privacy of their holdings."[21]

Charles G. Untermeyer, who served as director of presidential personnel in the early years of the George H. W. Bush administration, explained that the full range of ethics regulations contributed in a cumulative way to the disinclination of people to accept presidential appointments.

> It's the totality of all the disincentives that keeps people out of government. . . . [Low] pay is part of it—though I've never thought of that as number one, since everyone takes that for granted. . . . There's the financial disclosure requirement and the divestiture requirement. Then there are the post-government employment restrictions, which mean that some people can't return to the field from which they were recruited. With the post of under secretary of Defense for acquisitions, there are legends about the number of people they had to talk to in order to fill the job. This was a classic example of the post-employment problem: The person who holds this job deals with everything in the way of acquisitions. It would be hard to find a post-government employer he hadn't dealt with. [22]

Terrel H. Bell, who had served as an appointee before the passage of the Ethics in Government Act and then later returned to government as a cabinet secretary in the Reagan administration, described in his memoir an appointee's-eye view of the deterrent impacts of contemporary ethics policy.

> When a new administration takes over, the number of FBI background investigations soars, and a sizable backlog builds up. Candidates have to wait their turn. It is often a very long wait. In the meantime, the rumors proliferate and the candidate must have a very strong yearning for the job to withstand the emotional pressure and loss of privacy.
>
> Nor is that all. When the full-field investigation is completed, those close to the president and responsible for saving him from embarrassment usually send out trial balloons through the press to see if there will be any unanticipated political fight over the nomination. Often, only after a pending high-level appointment has been flaunted publicly will such opposition surface, despite all the clearances that have preceded it. . . . Usually it is only at this point that there are indications of a Senate confirmation fight instead of smooth sailing. This

is why "usually reliable sources" are quoted to the effect that so and so is under strong consideration for appointment by the president to X position in his administration. If criticism emerges and the appointment appears to be controversial, the president and his staff will weigh whether the candidate is worth a fight and the expenditure of political capital. It is not uncommon at this late juncture of the torturous appointment process for the poor soul to be dropped abruptly and without comment. Rumors have flown around in the press. Current employers are aware of the candidacy. The FBI has been busy poking about his or her neighborhood and place of work. Local, state, and national political leaders have been contacted. The consideration is a widely known "secret." To be abandoned after all this is obviously humiliating. It is a wonder our government attracts any talent at all to high positions.[23]

In April 1981, in the midst of the Reagan transition, Fred Fielding reflected on the impact of the Ethics in Government Act. He cited a number of examples of individuals whom the administration had failed to recruit because of the act.[24] Then he noted one of the residual effects of the deterrent effects that ethics policy has on those contemplating public service:

But there are more cases that you will never know about. Anyone interested in government must face the fact that over the years a very subtle effect will occur. The younger, mid-range person will not be attracted to government, or will feel the price is too high because he or she cannot come in at this time. The public has lost its ability not only to have their services but also, more important, the ability to call upon them in later life, when they might come back into a more responsible position at a higher level and bring with them that experience they gained earlier plus the experience they gained in the private sector. In essence, what we are doing is ruining the potential, for a certain level of citizen-statesmen, public servants, who traditionally go in and out of public service. This is a problem that I feel is real, and has been given little or no consideration.

. . . The point where a law designed to protect the public becomes the very obstacle to providing the public with the most competent people for public service is where the law ceases to fulfill its purpose. The law then is not serving the people. The people are then not being served by their very laws.[25]

Where the Rubber Meets the Road

Those who have had hands-on experience as presidential recruiters have a broad view of the barriers that ethics policy poses to attracting talented presidential appointees. But the most worrisome impediments are experienced in recruiting for certain kinds of positions. Most personnel directors find little difficulty in recruiting for the most senior positions: cabinet secretaries, major agency heads, and high-visibility ambassadorships, for example. Those positions have an inherent appeal that overcomes diminished salaries, lost privacy, high stress, and long hours. Some people call it "psychic income," the prestige that comes from being at the center of important public affairs. Supporters of contemporary ethics policy tend to belittle the impacts on appointees by pointing out that what they gain from public service far outweighs what they sacrifice in income and privacy to undertake it.

But most appointed positions in the executive branch provide little psychic income. They are at the periphery of public view and no one who fills those posts becomes a celebrity for doing a good job. Many of the positions filled by presidential appointments are scientific or technical in character. They are usually filled by substantive specialists. Box 6-1 lists a small sample of those positions.

In filling positions such as these the burden of ethics policy is felt most heavily. Typically the people selected are not wealthy. Most have worked in research labs, universities, or the technical side of corporations. Often their salaries in the private sector are very close in amount to what they would earn as presidential appointees.[26] And while most candidates for these jobs could endure government salaries, they find it much harder to cope with the loss of other income required by ethics policy: royalties from their writings, outside earned income, consulting, teaching, and so on.

"The science and technology positions have been the hardest to fill," Charles G. Untermeyer, chief personnel recruiter in the George H. W. Bush administration, told *Science* magazine, "because of the difficulty in finding able people who share the president's agenda and are willing to come to Washington to work for the pay and under the conditions which federal government service requires these days."[27]

Increasingly, as well, the high-quality technical people whom the government seeks to recruit are involved in entrepreneurial science and hold stock options and patent rights and other kinds of assets with high income potential that is diminished by compliance with the conflict-of-interest regulations.

Box 6-1. *Sample of Appointed Scientific and Technical Positions in the Federal Executive Branch*

Director, National Institute of Standards and Technology
Administrator, National Oceanic and Atmospheric Administration
Director of defense research and engineering
Assistant secretary of energy for fossil energy
Director, National Cancer Institute
Assistant secretary of the interior for water and science
Commissioner of labor statistics
Assistant secretary of state for oceans and international environmental and
    scientific affairs
Director, National Science Foundation
Assistant administrator for air and radiation, Environmental Protection
    Agency

And for these technical specialists, the post-employment rules are especially daunting. An expert of sonar technology may have limited employment opportunities outside the government where only a few companies work on sonar development and all of them have large government contracts.

The National Academy of Sciences, reflecting widespread concern in the scientific community about deterrents to government service, conducted two studies of ethics policy and the appointment process, one in 1992 and one in 2001. Both found the kinds of serious recruiting problems indicated in this statement from the 1992 report:

[The] in-and-out system of executive leadership for federal science and technology has served the nation well and should be carefully nurtured. Instead, a number of factors are making it harder to recruit highly qualified scientists, engineers, and medical experts from the private sector for top government leadership positions. The factors cited most often include: more stringent and confusing post-government employment restrictions; the longer, more burdensome, and more intrusive nomination and Senate confirmation process; stricter and more costly conflict-of-interest provisions; more detailed requirements for public financial disclosure.

. . . It is not only taking longer to fill key positions but it is also becoming harder to recruit top candidates. It is impossible to document the increasing rate of turndowns because most candidates drop out before a formal job offer is made, but panel members familiar with recent openings in the defense, energy, and health areas know of cases where it was necessary to go to the tenth, twentieth, and even thirtieth name on a list of desirable candidates. While some outstanding appointments have nevertheless been made, the reluctance of the most desirable candidates in recent years is disturbing.[28]

A study of Defense Department acquisition capability came to a similar conclusion in 1986. It noted the critical importance of getting talented executives to run the department's acquisition programs. But, noting a number of new ethics regulations, it concluded that "recruiting the most capable executives for jobs of such importance to the nation is extremely difficult, however, in the face of current disincentives to entering public service."[29]

One of the nation's leading students of the news media, Professor Larry J. Sabato, notes that it is not just the ethics rules but also the news coverage resulting from the open access to personal information they permit that affects recruitment.

> Simply put, the price of power has been raised dramatically, far too high for many outstanding potential officeholders. An individual contemplating . . . [public] office must now accept the possibility of almost unlimited intrusion into his or her financial and personal life. Every investment made, every affair conducted, every private sin committed from college years to the present may one day wind up in a headline or on television. For a reasonably sane and moderately sensitive person, this is a daunting realization, with potentially hurtful results not just for the candidate but for his or her immediate family and friends. To have achieved a nongovernmental position of respect and honor in one's community is a source of pride and security, and the risk that it could be destroyed by an unremitting and distorted assault on one's faults and foibles cannot be taken lightly. American society today is losing the services of many exceptionally talented individuals who could make outstanding contributions to the commonweal, but who understandably will not subject themselves and their loved ones to abusive, intrusive press coverage.[30]

In the fall of 2000, in an effort to assess more systematically the impacts on presidential recruiting of ethics policy and other aspects of the appointments process, the Presidential Appointee Initiative conducted a survey of people holding the kinds of positions in the private and independent sectors from which presidential appointees are normally recruited. We sought to identify people who would be in the on-deck circle for presidential appointments—senior executives of Fortune 500 corporations, university presidents, heads of large nonprofits, state and local government officials, prominent lobbyists, and visible specialists at think tanks. We queried them about their perceptions of the appointment process, the appeal of public service, and the likelihood they would join a presidential administration if asked.

One in five of the sample had been considered for appointment by a presidential administration. Of the group that had been considered, 21 percent were offered an appointment and declined to accept it and 32 percent would have declined an appointment had one been offered. That is to say that of those who had been under serious consideration for presidential appointments, more than half did decline or would have declined the appointment.[31]

When the entire sample of leaders was asked their opinions of the job of a presidential appointee, the vast majority thought it would be an honor to serve their country in these positions. But the practical realities of high-level public service were a troubling deterrent to many. Seventy-five percent believed that the salaries of presidential appointees were somewhat or much poorer than those for similar jobs in the private sector. More than two-thirds thought that public service would be much more or somewhat more disruptive to their lives than employment in the private sector.

More than half of the sample thought that the word "embarrassing" described the nomination and confirmation process well. Forty-two percent thought the selection and clearance process would be an "ordeal," and two-thirds thought the same of the Senate confirmation process. More than a third thought the jobs would be more attractive if the financial disclosure forms were easier to complete, 36 percent thought that "making the conflict of interest laws easier to meet" would make the jobs more attractive, and almost three quarters said they would find the jobs more attractive if the process of being appointed were simplified.

The authors of this study conclude:

America's civic and corporate leaders view the current process as unfair, confusing, and embarrassing. . . . The survey shows that the spirit of service is willing, but the process for entry is weak. To the extent the nation wants presidential appointees who represent the talent and wisdom that resides across the sectors covered in this report, it must address the persistent strains it places on appointees as they enter office.[32]

Winnowing

The impact of ethics policy and its attendant culture of purity on recruitment is felt in another way as well. It does not just deter good people from entering government service. It also places constraints on the kinds of people who can be considered for presidential appointments. The post-Watergate mentality has morphed into what one commentator has called a "purity potlatch."[33] We no longer expect people simply to perform honestly while in government. We expect that their entire lives before entering government are free of mistakes and controversy, no matter how minor, no matter how distant. And we have deployed an investigative dragnet, designed to ensure that no potential appointee makes it into government if he or she has ever done anything that might prove uncomfortable or embarrassing if publicized during the appointment process.

Presidential staff now routinely ask all candidates for appointment questions such as these:[34]

—Identify each instance in which you have testified orally or in writing before Congress in a nongovernmental capacity and specify the subject matter of each testimony.

—List each book, article, column, or publication you have authored and any speeches you have given.

—Have you ever been publicly identified either personally or by organizational membership with a particularly controversial national or local issue?

—Have you or your spouse ever had any association with any person, group, or business venture that could be used, even unfairly, to impugn or attack your character and qualifications for a government position?

—Is there any information, including information about members of your family, that could be considered a possible source of embarrassment to you, your family, or the president?

It is commonplace as well to subject candidates for appointment to lengthy interviews in which they are asked invasive questions about the most intimate details of their lives: about marital breakups, estranged children, psychiatric treatment, whether they have ever had an abortion. The purpose of this vetting is to get potential problems out in private before they come out in public. But it contributes to the prevailing mentality that it is rarely worth expending political capital on an appointment that might be controversial.

This mentality favors the bland over the bold. In the fast-moving world of the twenty-first century, those who succeed in enterprises outside government often do so by pushing against constraints and boundaries, by challenging conventional thinking, by wielding the sword of creative destruction that drives modern capitalism. Perhaps it was necessary to shrink a work force by laying off thousands of employees to turn a sick company around and make it profitable. Perhaps there was lengthy litigation when a business leader challenged an oppressive regulation. Perhaps a keen investor got rich quickly by seeing a market opportunity that no one else saw.

Those people, whatever the magnitude of their talents and whatever value they might add by bringing those talents to government, are not well designed for the modern appointment process. However appealing they might be as creative members of a contemporary administration, they are— in the prevailing political calculus—not worth the trouble their nominations might create.

So, much more often than we should, we get cabinet secretaries who are little more than caretakers, who disappear from public view more quickly than if they had gone into witness protection. The great bureaucratic movers and shakers of the past, the Harvey Wileys and Gifford Pinchots and Hyman Rickovers and Jim Webbs, are largely an extinct species now. And modern Supreme Court appointees are not the Louis Brandeises and Thurgood Marshalls and Felix Frankfurters who were at the forefront of important legal battles before they joined the court. Instead, they are lawyers whose principal qualification seems to be that they have toiled in competent obscurity and will not provoke controversy when their names are announced as the president's nominee. Northwestern University constitutional law professor Steven G. Calabresi explains the dynamic that led to this change.

> The reason the politics of ethical assault leads to mediocrity in judicial and high executive offices is clear: controversial people who might actually do something cause interest groups to launch a smear campaign to protect the status quo. Because any indiscretion, however minor and however long ago committed, is enough to trigger massive media coverage, all but the least controversial and least interesting individuals rapidly find themselves disqualified. This is particularly

the case because of the bizarre dynamics of the Senate confirmation process as covered by the press and by television. Major televised confirmation hearings are best thought of as an election in which the nominee is the only candidate and the vote is a choice of YES or NO on the nominee's entire life and career. There is no choice between two or three leading contenders each of them human and flawed as in a presidential, gubernatorial, or senatorial campaign. . . . The only individuals who can run this gauntlet successfully are those who are sufficiently indecisive, incompetent, or boring so that we can rest assured that no one will care whether they hold high office or not.[35]

Nobody Home

The ever-expanding burdens on new presidential appointees and the depressing effect these have on the ability of presidents to find talented people willing to accept these jobs is costly in yet another way. The staffing of new administrations grows slower and slower.

This book began with William O. Douglas's description of his entry into government service as head of the Securities and Exchange Commission in 1936. The transition from private to public sector or from one important government job to another was efficient and seamless in Douglas's time, as it had been for all of the history of the Republic until the 1950s. The president offered the job, the appointee accepted it, the nomination went to the Senate, and confirmation was usually swift and uncomplicated. The new appointee was on the job within weeks of the first contact. That process allowed new administrations to be up and running with something close to full staffing within eight to ten weeks of the new president's inauguration.

The contemporary reality could not be more different. Presidents over the last forty years have taken longer and longer to get their administrations in place. Figure 6-1 indicates the number of months after inauguration before the average appointee was confirmed by the Senate in these administrations.

In the George H. W. Bush and Clinton administrations, the average exceeds eight months. It was into the second year before either administration was close to fully staffed with Senate-confirmed appointees of its own choosing. The George W. Bush administration suffered similar delays in 2001. On the first anniversary of George W. Bush's inauguration, 160 of 508 (31 percent) important positions in the executive branch had not yet been filled by a Senate-confirmed Bush appointee.[36]

Figure 6-1. *Average Number of Months from Inauguration to Confirmation for Initial PAS Appointees, by Administration, 1961–93*

Months

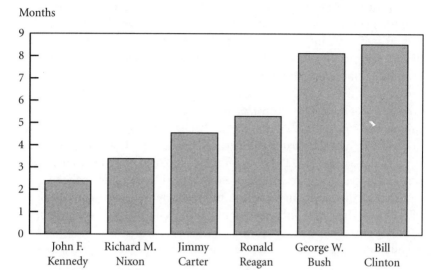

Administration

Source: Calculated from data in *Congressional Quarterly Almanac* (Washington: Congressional Quarterly) for 1961, 1969, 1977, 1981, and 1989. Data for Clinton administration are calculated from reports prepared by Rogelio Garcia, specialist in American national government, Government Division, Congressional Research Service. See *CRS Report to Congress: Presidential Appointments to Full-Time Positions in Executive Departments During the 103d Congress,* 93-736 GOV (Government Printing Office, revised December 29, 1993); and *CRS Report to Congress: Presidential Appointments to Full-Time Positions in Independent and Other Agencies, 103d Congress,* 93-924 GOV (Government Printing Office, revised December 30, 1993).

Note: Included in the calculation are positions filled by presidential appointment with Senate confirmation—so-called PAS appointees—in all of the cabinet departments and most of the large independent agencies. Regulatory commissioners, inspectors general, ambassadors, U.S. attorneys, and U.S. marshals are not included.

The time required to complete the staffing of new administrations has grown for several reasons. One is the steadily increasing numbers of positions now filled by presidential appointments that require Senate confirmation. Over recent decades, new laws have added to the number of positions at the top of the executive hierarchy, creating more undersecretaries and assistant secretaries, agency assistant directors, and so on, than ever before. The staffing task is harder, in part, because it is bigger.

But that explains only part of the delay. A more significant explanation is the accumulation of new steps that have been added to the appointment process or the elaboration of some traditional steps, all for the purpose of examining the character and past behavior—that is to say, the ethical qualifications—of contemporary appointees. The William O. Douglases of the past did not have to undergo FBI full-field investigations, did not have to fill out multiple forms and questionnaires answering hundreds of questions about the smallest details of their lives, did not have to make a full and accurate accounting of their complete personal finances and those of their spouses and minor children, and did not have to sit through long interviews and answer questions about their medical history, psychiatric experiences, drug use, sexual activities, and so on. They were not fingerprinted, their tax records were not scrutinized, and everything they had ever written was not analyzed.

Nor was the Senate in Douglas's time usually under the control of the opposition party. Nor did senators and Senate committees have large staffs with the capacity to conduct their own investigations of nominees and thus require nominees to go through yet another round of forms and questionnaires for Senate purposes. Nor were many Senate confirmation hearings held in public and nominees themselves usually expected to testify.[37] By the end of the twentieth century, the Senate was taking four months on average to confirm presidential appointees after receiving their nominations from the White House.[38] This is twice as long as the average confirmation time in the 1960s.

The extraordinary time that it now takes to complete an appointment is time that comes out of the hide of the appointees who often linger for six months or more in the limbo of the process as well as of the new administration waiting for its appointees to arrive. The clock ticks eternally on and windows of political opportunity begin to close, but the new team is not yet on the field. In an insightful book about presidential policymaking, political scientist Paul C. Light wrote:

Why is the first year so important for the President's agenda? The answer rests on the cycle of decreasing influence. Presidents and staffs are painfully aware that their most valuable resources dwindle over the term. They understand that the essential resource, capital, evaporates over time, that the first year offers the greatest opportunity for establishing the domestic program. Though information and expertise are rarely at a peak in the first year, capital does not keep, and Presidents must take advantage of whatever momentum they have; to wait is to squander the most important advantage.[39]

Yet contemporary presidents find themselves least equipped to govern effectively at precisely the time in the lives of their administrations when opportunities for their leadership are ripest.

Health and Human Services secretary Tommy Thompson lamented the
loss of momentum for new administrations in a speech at the National
Press Club in April 2001.

> You have a new administration—and I am not being critical of one
> political party or another—I think it was the same for Clinton—I
> think it took him almost a year after he was first elected before he got
> his people approved. And it's going to be—you know, it's going to be
> a long period of time before our people are approved in this adminis-
> tration. But what a loss, you know, to have a department like Health
> and Human Services that is so large, that wants to do so much and is
> involved in so much, that we can't get our key people confirmed. . . .
>
> I think you know the system—and I went through the system. First
> you have to fill out a heck of a lot of paperwork for the president. And
> then you have the privilege of the FBI come and do a detailed back-
> ground. And, you know, they had 10 FBI agents in Wisconsin looking
> at me. . . .
>
> And then you get a chance to go through the confirmation hear-
> ings, which require new forms, because you're in the Department of
> Health and Human Services. You get the chance to go in front of two
> committees which wanted different forms and different applications
> and different things. One wanted all the bills that I introduced when I
> was a legislator and governor and all the ones I vetoed. Well, I hap-
> pened to veto more bills than all the other governors in the United
> States combined. So I had a huge file. And the other committee
> wanted all the speeches I had given. And over 35 years of speeches in
> public life is a lot. . . . And then after that you get to go through the
> hearings. And then after you get through with the hearings you get the
> privilege then to go in front of the ethics department. And because the
> Department of Health and Human Services is so widespread, every
> little bit of stock that you own is a potential conflict. So you get the
> privilege of selling all of your stock. . . .
>
> And so that's the system. And the system is too long, too detailed.
> And I am not blaming anybody or any party or anything, it's just that
> the process—you should not have to go through all of those steps in
> order to serve. And there should be a simpler way to do it. I know I—we

don't wait that long in state governments; you don't wait that long in private business. Only in the federal government does it take six to eight to nine months to get an assistant secretary or a secretary on the job. [40]

It is not only at the beginning of an administration that the effects of these delays are felt. Every administration has turnover among its appointees. These are difficult, exhausting jobs with high stress and long hours.[41] So the task of recruitment and appointment never stops. As the first round ends in the second year of a new administration, the second round begins. But in Washington, departing appointees rarely delay their departure until the arrival of their successors. They know too well how long that can take and they have other fish to fry.

As a consequence, a growing affliction for modern presidential administrations is the vacancy problem, the sizable percentage of top administration posts that have no confirmed appointee in them. The vacancy rate, according to several recent directors of presidential personnel, sometimes exceeds a quarter of all positions filled by presidential appointment with Senate confirmation—so-called PAS positions.[42] At the end of 1996, for example, there were vacancies in sixty-two positions in the executive departments, thirty-three in the independent agencies, and twenty-six on boards and commissions.[43] A study conducted in 1997 found the following:

—At the end of March 1997, nearly a quarter of PAS positions lacked a Senate-confirmed Clinton appointee. At the Labor Department, there were nine vacancies including the secretary among the nineteen positions at the top. At the Commerce Department, ten of twenty-nine senior positions were vacant.[44]

—In the middle of May 1997, nearly a third of the executive branch PAS positions had no current, confirmed appointee in them. At the State Department, three undersecretary and five assistant secretary positions lacked Senate-confirmed incumbents. There was neither a permanent director nor a deputy at the Federal Aviation Administration.[45]

—In the first week of August 1997, 46 of the 109 positions on boards and commissions were vacant.[46] At the Federal Communications Commission, four of the five seats were vacant or filled by incumbents whose departure was pending. On the National Labor Relations Board, two of the five seats were vacant and two were held by recess appointees. The Food and Drug Administration had been without a commissioner since the departure of David Kessler seven months earlier.

—At the end of August 1997, 30 percent of the top political jobs in the administration remained unfilled for the second term.[47]

A study by the General Accounting Office covering the period from November 21, 1998, to June 30, 2000, found that on average nearly 20 percent of the PAS positions in the federal government were vacant during that time. Some stood vacant for half a year or more.

It is hard to imagine any organization operating at anything near peak efficiency with a fifth to a third of its top positions vacant. In the federal government, vacant positions are often filled temporarily by acting officials, usually lower-level appointees or members of the senior executive service. At some times in recent years there have been more people in acting positions in Washington than in Hollywood. An acting official is a deer on ice—working as hard to stay upright as to move forward. Gail Wilensky, who served as acting head of the Health Care Financing Administration in the George H. W. Bush administration, points out that "it's difficult for an acting leader to have the negotiating and bargaining positions that an approved presidential appointee has. There's no question it's a problem." And Don Wortman, who held several acting positions during his career as a senior civil servant, said, "As acting administrator, there are things you can't get resolved: responses to Congress on complex issues, court cases involving the agency, difficult regulatory decisions. You don't have the clout. People work around you. Or they wait."[48]

Acting officials have little latitude to make important decisions, to initiate new policies, and to manage their agencies with the full force of the presidency behind them. They command less respect and exercise less influence within their agencies, within the administration more broadly, and on Capitol Hill than would a confirmed appointee. A government run by acting officials is like a Broadway play with understudies filling in for the leads: the songs get sung, the dances get danced, the curtain comes down, but something critical is missing. If staffing with acting officials were a good way to run a country, government could dispense completely with the appointment process. But it is not.

Hidden Costs

The new regulations have yet another cost, one rarely included in discussions of ethics policy. But it is a significant cost, and it has become steadily more apparent over the years since the 1970s when the two major political parties began to accommodate to the growing frequency of divided government. These costs manifest themselves primarily in three ways.

The Investigatory Culture

The first hidden cost of the ethics policy is the emergence of an investigatory culture in American politics. Everybody seems to be investigating somebody all the time. Candidates for administration jobs are investigated before they become appointees. Administration officials are investigated after they are in office: by their own inspectors general, by Congress, by independent counsels, by investigative reporters. Members of Congress are investigated by each other, by their ethics committees, by the Justice Department. The FBI, the U.S. attorneys, and other police and prosecutors have hundreds of investigations ongoing at any moment.

New initiatives in ethics policy have accelerated the establishment of this investigatory culture by working from the premise that the best way to prevent ethics violations is to investigate anyone who might be in a position to commit such a violation even before there is a hint of venality and then to create a small standing army of investigators ready to pounce at the slightest hint of impropriety. The investigators and prosecutors do not always wait for evidence before going to work. Sometimes they set up their own traps, called stings, to see if they can lure out the evil that lurks in the hearts of public employees.

C. Boyden Gray, who served as White House counsel in the George H. W. Bush administration, tells of one of his own brushes with the investigatory culture:

> There was the question of my stock in a number of different organizations, one of which was Brown and Root Construction, which was bought by Haliburton, which was bought by somebody else. I owned stock in the underlying company at some point when I filed my disclosure form, but by the time I got engaged in some activity which sought to have some implication to all of this, I had long since sold the stock. But the forms don't provide for instantaneous updating. The press got into it. I was the subject, solely, individually, of a whole two-day hearing in the House of Representatives about stock that I had sold.
>
> And then there were the questions about whether deferred compensation that I was to receive should have been reported in Column B instead of Column C. This was the subject—this problem was the

subject of four days of intensive front-page *New York Times* scrutiny. And, I repeat, the only question was whether the deferred compensation should have been reported in Column B as an asset rather than Column C, as income.

Did it really matter? I was disqualified from the subject matter of the compensation in any event, but never mind, it was the subject of four days of intensive press coverage designed, I think, to knock me out of office for some reasons that had nothing to do with ethics. But this is what happens, and we have these wars and have these games that get played and that is a total distortion of what goes on.[49]

Once the investigatory momentum is in place, it becomes difficult to stop or control. Investigators investigate. That is their job. If they do not have real crimes or clear evidence of impropriety, they investigate something else. Every new kind of impropriety inspires new kinds of investigations and usually calls for reinforcements. The necessity and value of the investigative machinery that has grown from the evolution of ethics policy over the past few decades have never been seriously questioned or challenged. A moment has never arisen when careful policy analysts or fiscal disciplinarians have declared that there are more investigators and more investigations than a prudent government needs. The mood of the times has always inclined the process in the opposite direction. Investigation is a good thing, a desirable protection of public integrity. The best way to ensure that we have honest leaders is to keep them honest by constant scrutiny of their actions and their character.

But over time this attitude is corrosive. It keeps good people out of government or drives good people out sooner than necessary. It forces federal employees to adopt postures of caution and defensiveness, to avoid decisions or actions—however desirable for other reasons—that might incur charges of self-dealing or conflict of interest or something else that would provoke an investigation and an assault on their character.

The investigatory culture also adds measurably to bureaucratic inefficiency. To ensure that no employee misbehaves, that not one federal dollar is misspent or unaccounted for, we build massive duplication into the decisionmaking systems. Procedures and agencies themselves are overcentralized; everything requires multiple approvals. There is constant oversight, internal and external. Paperwork piles up, as agencies issue report after report to other agencies, to Congress, to the public. Every decisionmaking process is thickened and slowed by the measures taken to eliminate every possibility of conflict of interest, abuse of office, or other ethical violations. And because all of this requires more staff, the agencies of government thicken at the top and in the middle. More people are added to review the work of people already on board.

Weapons of Partisan Combat

The second hidden cost of the ethics policies is the role they have come to play in partisan combat. In the days when winning elections usually meant that one party had a few years in which to run the government without constant interference and interruption by the other party, when loyal opposition meant asking hard questions and challenging assumptions and policy directions but little more, most partisan combat took place in the electoral process.

But no more. Partisan combat never ends. Elections are simply benchmarks in ongoing struggles between the political parties for control of the policymaking process. The new motto seems to be: If you cannot beat your opponent in an election, beat up on your opponent after the election. And there have never been better weapons for beating up on opponents than those the ethics regulations provide.

When a candidate is elected president, the opposition party can slow the staffing of the victor's administration by questioning and investigating the ethics of his nominees. When an appointee is in place, the opposition can leap on some hint of ethical impropriety and call for the appointment of an independent counsel or demand a Justice Department investigation or initiate congressional hearings. When the investigatory committees of Congress are in the hands of the opposition party, the investigations of an administration and its officials rarely stop.

And then the television lights come on. Ethics investigations are show business. Televised hearings are mecca for publicity-hungry members of Congress and for the anxious producers of the twenty-four-hour all-news networks. Reporters spend hours waiting in front of courthouses and in the driveways of the subjects of these investigations, waiting for a few words that will get them on the evening news.

Rarely do the investigations and the endless public attention yield legal violations or ethical indiscretions equal to the intense news storms they generate. The twenty independent counsel investigations cost more than $200 million and filled thousands of columns of newspaper copy, but only seven of them resulted in any convictions, and some of those were later overturned on appeal. All the hand-wringing about the mobsters Labor

Secretary Ray Donovan may or may not have associated with produced no convictions. When he was cleared of the charges of racketeering against him, he held a press conference and asked plaintively, "Which office do I go to to get my reputation back?" Far fewer reporters attended the press conference and worried about Donovan's reputation than had pursued stories of the Donovan scandal when the topic was hot. Years of investigations stemming from conspiracy theories about the death of Vincent Foster, deputy counsel to President Clinton, only confirmed the official explanation that he had committed suicide because he was overwhelmed beyond coping by the character of Washington life—a city, Foster wrote, where "ruining people is considered sport."[50] A president was impeached and brought to trial in the Senate, tying up the government for nearly two years, primarily for doing what hundreds of thousands of Americans do every year: denying marital infidelity.

But the investigatory culture does not require much substance to be the best show in town. President Clinton said of the appointment process: "The climate has changed to the point where a lot of people don't want to fool with it any more. Somebody raises a question, then there's a presumption of guilt. You have to prove yourself innocent of things you're not even sure what the charge is."[51]

We have come to expect a level of perfection in our public servants that few of us expect in ourselves, our friends, or the members of our families. And with all the rigid regulations that now compose federal ethics policy, we have armed those who wish to embarrass and thus weaken their political opponents with wonderfully effective weapons for that purpose.

Presidential Millstone

A third hidden cost of contemporary ethics policy is the harm it does to the capacity for presidential leadership. One cannot help but note the irony in this, for much of this harm is self-inflicted. Presidents have been the leading cheerleaders for new ethics regulations in a regularly repeated effort to demonstrate the high standards of their administrations.

President John F. Kennedy called for a recodification and revitalization of ethics standards in 1961. President Lyndon B. Johnson established a code of conduct, required confidential reports of personal finances, and created the appearance standard in 1965. President Jimmy Carter introduced legislation that came to be the Ethics in Government Act of 1978. President George H. W. Bush banned outside earned income for his appointees and established new standards of conduct. He introduced legislation that added more layers of regulation and constraint. President Clinton extended the post-employment prohibitions to five years.

In their contributions to ethics policy, presidents have helped weaken the presidency in at least two ways. First, they have made it harder to recruit talented people into their administrations and, by lengthening the appointment process, have slowed the effective start of their administrations. But, second, and more important, they have given weapons to their political and ideological enemies that have been used to weaken the capacity of any president to lead the country.

Even when presidents themselves have escaped the scrape of the ethics lance, it has struck other people in their administrations with negative impacts on the president. An administration with appointees or aides under investigation is always weakened. Instead of White House stories about the president's policy proposals or the president's arguments for initiatives he supports, the reporters on the north lawn talk about scandals and the president's reaction to scandals. Does the president support the wounded appointee or nominee? Has he asked for a resignation? Will he stand by the nomination? America wants to know.

It does not take many of these scandals before the shine on a new administration begins to tarnish. Jimmy Carter came to the White House in the shadow of Watergate promising he would never lie to the American people and that he would provide them a president as good as they were. But then there were questions about OMB director Bert Lance's banking practices in Georgia, about the integrity of the president's own brother, and then the first independent counsels were appointed to investigate charges of illegal drug use by the president's chief of staff and another senior aide. The charges turned out to be groundless, but that did not mitigate much of the damage. The bloom was off the rose.

Ethics policy creates ample opportunity for a president's opponents to keep an administration on the defensive. There may be no significant misbehavior, no provable offenses. But it is a simple matter now to produce smoke, even in the absence of fire. And that kind of smoke screen makes it hard for the president to communicate with the American people about substantive issues of importance and makes it hard for the American people to accept the president's words at face value.

In the American political system, the president's effective power is rooted as much in the capacity for publicity and persuasion as in the Constitution. The bully pulpit matters just as much, often more, than the specifics of Article II. And anything that diminishes the president's ability to command the attention of the American people, to get a fair and open-minded reaction from them, to convince them that his proposals and initiatives are in the public interest weakens him.

Some students of the presidency have argued that presidents are more prominent than powerful. But that is not quite right. They can be very powerful when they can use their prominence to serve their purposes. But that becomes exceedingly difficult when the president and his people are the subjects of constant investigation of frequent—and frequently scurrilous—assaults on their integrity, when the White House has to spend so much time defending its honor that there is little time left to do its business.

"Presidential power is by its nature at least somewhat charismatic," argues Steven G. Calabresi. "It depends on the moral authority and reputation of the President himself."

> Because the President is a national media figure and, in some ways, a giver of sermons to the American People, his truthfulness, uprightness, commitment to principle, and personal friendships are all subjects of intense public interest. . . .
>
> The political use of ethics probes as weapons strikes at the very heart of the moral authority that is vital to presidential power. By raising questions and doubts that are far easier to sow than they are to put to rest, the politics of ethical assault corrodes the very foundation of the modern presidency. The greater the number of charges, the graver the political damage that is done. . . . The net effect is a tremendous incentive for out-of-power groups to destroy a presidency early on by attempting to "smear" the President and his closest advisors, associates, friends and relatives.
>
> . . . The increasing political use of ethics probes is one of many developments in recent years which have disproportionately weakened the presidency and the executive branch of government.[52]

In practical terms there is little difference between scandal and charges of scandal. They generate the same amount of news. They require the same intensity of response. They are equally damaging to presidents and to the effective performance of presidential functions. The steady expansion of new ethics regulations and new legions of enforcers has greatly increased the opportunities for leveling such charges against a president or the people in his administration. There are more rules to violate, spiraling standards of conduct, more venues for investigation, and more investigators. It matters little how vigilant a president may be in his own behavior or in selecting honest subordinates. There is no place to hide from political enemies when they are crusading for ethics.

Conclusion

Very little real debate has taken place about the expansion of ethics regulations. A small band of congressional doubters questioned the wisdom of the Ethics in Government Act of 1978 when it was under consideration. And over the years, a handful of books questioned the value of the ethics policies. But the overwhelming sentiment has been that ethics regulation produces a higher level of ethical performance and is therefore good. At few points along the forty-year trail to contemporary ethics policy has there ever been much concern with the costs of that policy.

These costs, however, have been significant. The dollar costs of implementing and enforcing the ethics policies have grown steadily. One would be hard-pressed to name many other areas of public policy where so much money and so many people chase so little proven policy impact.

Furthermore, there are many other costs, not measurable by dollars. Our ethics policies have made it harder to recruit talented public officials, have made their government experience far more burdensome and unpleasant, and have slowed the staffing of new administrations. Government itself has become more difficult as partisans have learned to use new ethics regulations as weapons of political combat. And all of this has placed new burdens on the presidency and its institutional capacity for leadership.

So there is more to an analysis of ethics policy than a mere review of its benefits. As the political scientist Edward C. Banfield noted, "In governmental organization the costs of preventing or reducing corruption are not balanced against the gains with a view to finding an optimal investment. Instead corruption is thought of (when it comes under notice) as something that must be eliminated no matter what the cost."[53]

CHAPTER SEVEN

Lessons

We begin with a reminder of what we set out to accomplish here. An accelerating momentum in the final few decades of the twentieth century produced a steadily more comprehensive, elaborate, and rigid scheme for regulating the ethical behavior of federal employees. This accumulation of decisions became, though it was rarely explicitly cast as such, federal ethics policy. The task we set for ourselves was to apply standard techniques of policy analysis to try to determine whether, on balance, this has been good public policy.

The usual measure of a successful public policy is that it substantially achieves its stated objectives without generating significant, unintended, negative side effects. An unsuccessful policy is one that fails to substantially achieve its objectives or achieves some of its objectives but, in so doing, produces a new set of unanticipated problems that outweigh its benefits.

What can we then conclude about federal ethics policy? Where does the balance fall when the costs and benefits of the expansion in ethics regulation are weighed? Has the integrity of federal executive employees been elevated sufficiently to justify the costs of the regulatory effort and the burdens these regulations impose on individual employees and on government operations? Is there a better way to ensure honest government in Washington, D.C.?

Costs and Benefits Redux

Is there more integrity in government today than there was before 1961?

No one knows because no one can measure what cannot be observed. The daily activities of the millions of people who work in the federal executive branch, or the several thousand who are presidential appointees, cannot be tracked. The press tries, in a sense, but its tracking instruments are episodic and inconsistent. And reporters and editors and producers have an obvious bias: They are much more interested in dishonesty than in honesty. Scandal is what sells their products, and they are drawn to even the hint of scandal like moths to a flame. Press reports provide a measure of only one thing: the frequency of press reports about ethical impropriety. They do not serve as an indication of the level of ethical impropriety—or propriety.

The same problem arises when relying on measures of legal activity in the justice system. The number of investigations conducted, of prosecutions brought forward, of convictions achieved, would be helpful measures if all government behavior were subject to the same scrutiny and consistent decisionmaking about when to launch an investigation, when to proceed with a prosecution, when to convict. But there is no more consistency in measures of activity in the justice system than in the press. Some improprieties are observed and yield investigations; others do not. Some investigations lead to prosecutions; others do not. Some prosecutions produce convictions; others do not.

Further complicating the value of measures of legal activity are the changing standards of rule and law. Much of what is now defined as improper or illegal was once accepted practice. There are more rules and laws regulating the ethical behavior of public employees than ever before. And there are more agencies and more people enforcing those new rules and laws. One would expect significant increases in the number of investigations, prosecutions, and convictions even if there were no change in behavior because more behavior is now proscribed by law and more enforcement resources exist.

We have proceeded nonetheless in the face of these empirical challenges to try to assess the ethical behavior of federal employees and the integrity of government operations. We reviewed the improper and illegal activities of the Watergate bandits, the actions that yielded the post-Watergate mentality that has been a stimulus for so much of the new ethics policy. We found that while bad behavior was widespread during Watergate, little of it was of a kind that would have been deterred or prevented by most of the new regulations subsequently imposed. Most of those rules seek to prevent public employees from self-dealing and self-enrichment, from placing their self-interest above the public interest when they make official decisions.

But little that occurred during Watergate was about self-dealing. Most of the Watergate crimes were violations of law aimed at subverting the political process and the constitutional rights of American citizens. They were crimes seeking political advantage substantially more than personal financial gain. Almost nothing in the Ethics in Government Act of 1978 would have prevented most of those crimes.

Most laws are designed to address specific problems—to solve the problems or to prevent their recurrence. When the air was too dirty, for example, laws were enacted to clean it up and minimize further pollution. But many of the laws and executive orders that have contributed to contemporary ethics policy have failed in two ways to do this. First, they have been grounded in imprecise and often inaccurate assumptions about the behavior of government employees and, second, they have rarely produced regulations that fit the crimes they sought to prevent.

When President Dwight D. Eisenhower ordered the FBI to conduct background investigations of candidates for presidential appointments, he did so for national security purposes, to ensure that no security risks would find their way into important government posts. He could not have imagined that the FBI background investigations would grow to cover every appointed position, full or part time, international or domestic. Nor could he have imagined that what was intended as a national security review would evolve into a full-scale investigation of personal character and individual ethics.

The number of documented security risks in appointed positions in the federal government, even in the early 1950s, was substantially smaller than the Joseph McCarthys of the time alleged. In those days of passionate fear-mongering, the FBI security investigations probably provided more political value to the president than security value to the government.

When President Lyndon B. Johnson instituted the requirement for confidential financial disclosure by senior federal employees in 1965 and established the appearance standard for employee conduct, he was responding to no apparent problem in government. There had been no prominent instance of self-dealing by any federal employee whose behavior would have been different if he had previously disclosed his personal finances to the Civil Service Commission. Nor had there been any outbreak of bad appearances, of employees abiding by the letter of the ethics laws but appearing to act improperly. These additions to ethics policy were simply part of the

standard presidential leapfrog of trying to appear above reproach by imposing higher standards than one's predecessors. Again, the purpose was more
political than practical.

When Jimmy Carter proposed a sweeping ethics act to Congress and
huge majorities in both houses went along, there was no meaningful com-
parison of policy to practice, no careful assessment of need. One reads
through the entire legislative history of the Ethics in Government Act in
search of any kind of empirical analysis of the ethical behavior of federal
employees, some tally of indiscretion, illegality, or even bad appearances.
But there is none. The testimony taken by the congressional committees
with jurisdiction over this legislation reads like the stories from the sawdust
trail at an evangelist's revival meeting: We are all sinners and we need some
greater force to protect us from our own sinful impulses. Rarely in the history of American public policy has the burden of proof been so lightly
applied.

When President George H. W. Bush led a further tightening of the screws
with an executive order and more quickly enacted legislation, it may have
served the intended purpose of distancing his administration from a tainted
predecessor. But, again, the commission he appointed to formulate these
new policy initiatives was dominated by lawyers and produced a report
focusing on legal technicalities.[1] To students of federal ethics policy, that
was just another chapter in an old story. As Frank Anechiarico and James B.
Jacobs have noted,

> A frequent component of anticorruption politics is the impaneling of
> a "nonpolitical" independent commission to conduct an investigation
> and make recommendations for change; appointment of a nonparti-
> san blue ribbon panel is meant to calm public indignation and legiti-
> mate the authority of the government and political system with its
> integrity under attack. The commission, staffed by lawyers, often with
> prosecutorial experience, frames the problem in terms of inadequate
> rules and/or enforcement mechanisms. It inevitably proposes new
> laws to increase the costs of corrupt behavior and to make corruption
> more difficult to carry out. It often recommends the creation of new
> agencies or the reorganization of old ones.
>
> Social problems increasingly are approached as puzzles to be solved
> through comprehensive legal strategies. Currently, these strategies
> include prohibiting innocuous activities that are believed to provide
> the means or stepping stones to corrupt behavior. When corruption

recurs, failure is attributed to poor drafting and not enough law; typically the solution is "smarter" legal interventions. Some reformers have an extraordinary belief in the efficacy of legal threats to deter corrupt behavior; others cynically recognize that the best way to deal with scandals is to paper them over with ineffective laws that are not meant to be enforced.[2]

Before Bill Clinton even came to office in 1993 he had decided that the post-employment regulations did not go far enough, and he required all of his appointees to make a contractual agreement to abide by those restrictions for five years, not simply the one or two required by law. In the more than two decades those regulations had been in effect, they had rarely been breached. If there was a shred of evidence that the time periods embedded in the post-employment rules were too short to keep the government honest, it was never identified or cited by the new president. Again, this was a political measure designed without careful analysis of its necessity or cost. Its sole aim was to make the new administration appear more ethical than its predecessors.

One of the reasons, then, that government integrity may not have been enhanced by most of the regulations enacted under the ethics banner is that few of them followed any analysis of problems or careful study of the consequences they would yield. We should not be surprised if we found that a policy not carefully targeted at identifiable and measurable problems missed the target. Nor should we be surprised to find few indicators that government integrity has been substantially improved by these policies when we had so few indicators that it was in bad repair before we initiated them. If the policies seem to have had little effect, it may be because the margin for improvement was so small.

We must also beware of the trap into which many analysts fall of confusing policy output with policy outcome. Too often we measure the tangible things that policy has produced, assume their value, and substitute that for a more penetrating assessment of policy impact. We build a national highway system to enhance national security and interstate commerce, for example. But soon we start reporting the miles of new roads as a measure of success, not improvements in security or dollars added to commerce.

We undertook new ethics policies to raise the level of public integrity in government and to enhance public faith and confidence in that integrity. But public integrity and public confidence are hard to measure, hard to assess. And because policy outcomes are difficult to assess empirically, many of the commentaries on ethics policy are built instead on measures of policy output: how many financial disclosure forms are filed every year, how many appointees have divested stock or resigned from boards of directors, how many inspector general investigations have been launched, how many independent counsels have been appointed, how many convictions the Public Integrity Section has secured, how many investigators and prosecutors across the government are now in hot pursuit of federal employee misbehavior.

But do these really measure integrity in government or enhancements in public confidence? Probably not. They measure activities undertaken to accomplish those objectives, but not the state of accomplishment.

Benefits

We have sought to look beyond the output measures to assess outcomes. And we can find little evidence that government integrity is greater today than it was when this movement to expand federal ethics policy began more than four decades ago. The number of prosecutions and convictions of government employees charged with various forms of corruption has marginally increased. But those numbers are miniscule compared with the size of the federal work force. And how could there not be increases in prosecutions with so many new prosecutors and so many new laws to prosecute under?

More government employees go through the annual task of reporting the details of their personal finances to the government, almost a quarter million of them. More than twenty thousand file their reports for public disclosure. These requirements were intended to impose a kind of accountability by allowing the public and its agents to study the personal finances of federal employees to be sure they were not doing anything in public service that would add to their own enrichment.

But this has become one of the great empty rituals in all of American life. Almost no one looks at any of these reports. Our analysis found that most of the confidential reports get a quick review from an agency ethics officer before they are consigned to six years of dust collection. And of the 126,116 reports filed for public disclosure between 1995 and 2000, those of only 405 individuals were ever viewed by any member of the public, 26 percent of those by a single researcher who was studying ambassadors for purposes unrelated to ethics.

By these standards, a significant uptick was seen in examination of the public disclosure forms filed by George W. Bush administration appointees in 2001, with 1,887 requests. One might view this as evidence of renewed efforts to enforce a higher level of government integrity. But our analysis found that more than a third of those requests came from the Democratic National Committee or a labor union. We are skeptical that public integrity was their primary motive. We expect that political embarrassment and harassment, digging for politically fertile dirt, was the primary motive for these examinations. It always has been.

Proponents of the public disclosure requirement have argued that it does not matter who looks at the financial disclosure forms, in what numbers or for what purpose. What matters, they suggest, is that public employees go through the discipline of disclosure so they know what assets they hold and are made aware of potential conflicts of interest. This, it is further argued, has the added benefit of inspiring good behavior in response to the "suspicion of being watched."

Perhaps, but we know of no way to prove or demonstrate either benefit. We doubt seriously that many of the people qualified for high-level federal posts need some annual, externally mandated discipline to inform themselves of what financial assets they hold. Nor does it seem very likely to us, given the significant criminal penalties for self-dealing and conflict of interest, that the "suspicion of being watched" adds much deterrent effect.

But defenders of the public disclosure requirement might reply, "Perhaps a deterrent effect can't be proven empirically, but what's to hurt by requiring some disclosure? Isn't it just an insurance policy?" That is the right question: What is the harm?

One other goal of ethics policy is the enhancement of public confidence in government. There are no perfect measures of public confidence. In our time, public attitudes are usually measured by public opinion polls. No consistent, longitudinal set of poll questions is available asking a national sample about their level of confidence in the integrity of government.

But there are surrogates. Most notably, the American National Election Studies (ANES) biennially asks citizens about their trust in government. In addition, other questions focusing on similar dimensions of public opinion have appeared episodically in other national polls.

Nothing in any of this evidence could possibly yield the conclusion that public confidence in the integrity of the federal government is higher today than it was before most of the ethics policies were enacted. The most reliable measure, the ANES trust in government index question, indicates a steady decline in trust in government from the early 1960s when it rose above 60 percent to the end of the twentieth century when it fell below 30 percent.

It cannot be determined from this simple measure what caused this decline in trust in government. But it can certainly be determined that thousands of pages of new ethics laws and regulations did little to stop the decline. Perhaps trust in government would have fallen even lower without the new ethics policies. Their defenders sometimes offer this argument. The argument cannot be disproved—except, perhaps, to ask how much lower trust in government could possibly have fallen beyond the unimaginably low levels it reached in the last two decades of the twentieth century.

All of this is to say that the benefits of the new ethics policies are empirically unproven. No meaningful measure shows that government integrity is greater than it was before these policies were enacted. And every measure indicates that public confidence in the federal government is lower than it was. We have vastly expanded the *outputs* by ethics policy—the number and detail of rules, the constraints on federal employees, the number of enforcers and measures of their activity—but we can offer no similar expansion of the positive *outcomes* of ethics policy. More government integrity and more public confidence in government, the twin goals of the ethics policy, have not been accomplished.

Costs

Even if some significant benefits from new ethics policy initiatives could be discerned, they must be compared with the costs of the initiatives before making a summary judgment about the success of these policies. Accomplishment matters, but so does cost, in any policy analysis.

We identified several different kinds of costs in our review of contemporary ethics policy. The most obvious of those are the dollar costs, the money the federal government spends to implement its efforts to regulate the ethical behavior of federal employees. However, responsibility for the implementation of these policies is spread widely over the federal government—nearly every agency has some portion of this responsibility—and many of the people who manage ethics policies have other, unrelated responsibilities as well. For example, every agency has a designated agency ethics official, a DAEO. In some of the larger departments and agencies, the DAEO has something approaching full-time responsibilities for managing the department's ethics training and oversight programs. In smaller agencies, however, DAEOs are often lower-level attorneys in the counsel's office for whom ethics duties are only part of a broader portfolio of responsibilities. Similarly, some agencies in the ethics edifice spend only part of their time on ethics matters. The U.S. attorneys prosecute some public corruption cases, but again only as part of a larger set of responsibilities.

Because of these inconsistencies, measuring the full cost of managing federal ethics policy is difficult. But even relying on cost data from just those agencies that play the central roles in ethics policy, we find significant annual investments. We estimated that the cost of running the major ethics agencies in fiscal year 2000 was tens of millions of dollars for just the functions directly related to implementing and enforcing ethics policy. If we were to add to that the expenditures by other agencies on ethics policy, we believe the total cost would be significantly larger.

There is no objective basis for determining whether this kind of spending is justified or not. One can only make that determination by comparing what is spent with what is gained as a consequence of those expenditures. The ethics policy has several other costs, but all of them defy monetization. They include the burdens of time and effort imposed on hundreds of thousands of federal employees required to make a complete report each year on the details of their personal finances. We estimate that 342,198 hours or 57,033 person days are spent each year by federal employees in complying with this requirement.[3] The burden falls especially heavily on new presidential appointees who are now required to go through an intensive and invasive scrutiny that has no precedent in U.S. history and no analog in any other country in the world.

Then there is the recruiting burden the ethics requirements impose on American presidents. While the character of the recruitment process makes it impossible to measure this burden statistically, the overwhelming weight of anecdotal and testamentary evidence indicates that the overall burden is significant and that it strikes especially hard when presidents try to recruit the best of the country's scientific and technical talent to appointed positions in the public service. We have talked over many years with scores of people who have participated in the presidential appointments process. Not a single one of those ever stated that his or her job was easier because of federal ethics policies. Many, however, have argued just the opposite: that every new layer of ethics regulation diminishes the willingness of talented people to pay the price of public service. So while convincing good people to accept a presidential invitation to public service is harder than ever, the recruiters themselves feel constrained to avoid choosing candidates who might be extraordinary public officials but who are too controversial to get through the appointments process without significant difficulty or expenditure of presidential political capital.

Added to this is the burden that ethics policy imposes on new presidents at the outset of their administrations. By helping to elongate the appointments process beyond all reason, these policies have steadily slowed the start-up of new administrations. In the typical case now, it is well into an administration's second year before most of the appointed positions are filled with a confirmed appointee. This weakens the president's ability to take the policy initiative opportunity that occurs at the outset of a new administration and it handicaps efforts to respond at full strength to crises. When the terror attacks occurred on September 11, 2001, nearly nine months into the George W. Bush administration, 35 percent of the anti-terrorism and emergency response positions at the top of the federal executive branch did not yet have a confirmed appointee.[4]

Costs also are incurred by the use of the ethics regulations as weapons of political combat. Political analysts often describe the contemporary time as the era of the endless campaign, when elections are little more than minor benchmarks in ongoing policy struggles between competing parties and ideologies. A democratic theorist would argue that elections ought to give one group of leaders a mandate to govern for a period of time, at the end of which they should be held accountable by the voters for their leadership. If the voters like what they have seen, they can reelect those leaders. If they are unhappy, they can throw out the incumbents and get new leaders. Democracies are designed to work that way.

But that is about as far from an accurate description of what currently happens in American politics as one could get. Elections rarely offer clear policy choices to voters, and voters often respond by electing a president of one party and a Congress controlled by the other. Instead of getting out of the way so the winners can govern, the losers begin guerilla operations that never cease, using every weapon and every opportunity to attack, harass, embarrass, and otherwise weaken those who hold office. If you cannot beat them in an election, current practice now suggests, then do everything in your power to keep the winners from governing and implementing their policy priorities.

In that environment, one could hardly imagine a better set of tools than the ethics regulations provide for attacking, harassing, embarrassing, and weakening incumbent officeholders. Ethics regulations provide endless opportunities for invasive scrutiny, for constant investigation, for discovering technical violations of law. And the impact of ethics policy on the presidential appointments process allows an administration's adversaries to keep important offices vacant for months for no reason other than policy or ideological disagreements with the president's nominees.

The other rarely mentioned cost is the deterioration of presidential leadership capacity that results from constant nibbling away by those adversaries who use the ethics laws to keep an administration on the defensive. No one ever proved, for example, that Bill Clinton did anything illegal in his own peripheral involvement in the original financial dealings that later came to be known as the Whitewater scandal. Yet that scandal remained a prominent news item for more than half of his tenure in office and cost him and his subordinates not only an enormous amount of their time and attention but also a loss of face and faith.

The Constitution creates a relatively weak chief executive. Presidents can be effective leaders only by creative exercise of their limited formal powers and by exceptional skill in the public aspects of their leadership. Much of what is called presidential power is, in fact, charismatic. "The prevalent impression of a President's public standing," wrote Richard E. Neustadt in his classic study of presidential power, "tends to set a tone and define the limits of what Washingtonians do for him or do to him."[5]

An admired and respected chief executive has potent advantages in seeking to influence the policymaking community. But when presidents are constantly harassed by niggling questions about their or their subordinates' ethics, when investigations into their behavior are the major news items for months, when every charge—however scurrilous—becomes the focus of endless analysis on talk radio and cable news channels, the capacity for charismatic leadership is gravely diminished.

The Road to Common Sense

Only wishful thinking could lead one to conclude that the benefits of federal ethics policy outweigh the costs. Surely no arrangement of the available evidence could yield that conclusion. The government has spent heavily on its ethics policies—in dollars and manpower, in burdens on individuals, in constraints on the quality of public management, and in deep corrosions of politics. The return has been little net gain in ethics and steady declines in public trust in government. The costs are too great, the benefits too scarce to sustain the current ethics policies. It is time to think about better ways to ensure the integrity of the public service without all the coincident costs that must be endured.

A good place to start is with the concept of what constitutes fitness for public service. American history is rich with examples of imperfect people who contributed mightily in public office. Presidents, members of Congress, and cabinet secretaries were unfaithful to their spouses, drank too much, and cursed and blasphemed in their private conversations. Some made awful mistakes in their lives before politics, and others became very successful in their private lives through actions that some people thought contemptible. The country enjoyed the benefits of their public service because the voters who elected them or the presidents and senators who appointed and confirmed them looked at the whole person and decided that they were fit for public service despite their human flaws or the controversy they inspired.

But in recent decades the notion of balanced judgments in assessing fitness for office has evolved into a far more rigid standard approaching perfection. Increasingly these days, no one who ever broke a law or drank to excess or violated marriage vows or pushed an envelope or did anything that might be controversial or an invitation to investigation need apply. But in adhering to the new standard, we lose the services of many good, though flawed, people whose election or appointment would improve government performance.

George W. Bush was an indifferent college student, had an undistinguished business career, has deep ties with the oil industry, drank heavily for much of his adult life, and has a conviction for driving while intoxicated. All of that was known to the American people who voted for him. They were able to compare those pieces of his persona with many other pieces and to decide that he was their best option. They made a balanced judgment.

But would a modern president have risked nominating a person with this kind of background to a senior appointive position? One can only imagine what details an FBI file might contain, what kinds of rumors opposing interest groups would float with friends in the communications media, what kinds of questions senators from the opposition party would pose at a confirmation hearing—if the nomination even made it to a hearing. A White House personnel officer might weigh all this and decide this was likely to be too controversial an appointment, not worth the battle it would require to win confirmation. A great deal is lost when this becomes the modus operandi.

One of the impacts of contemporary changes in ethics policy has been to criminalize, or legalize, much of what used to be regarded as political. In the past, for example, if members of a presidential administration were keeping company with representatives of powerful interest groups, there was some political risk in that. Opponents might criticize those cozy relationships, maybe even make an election issue out of it. But this was a matter for politics, not law.

Much of that has changed. Now laws require hundreds of thousands of government employees to reveal all of their personal financial connections. The kinds of contacts they can have with private interests are limited. The work they can do for such interests after they leave public service is proscribed in great detail. Now if there is a suggestion that a federal official is too cozy with the representative of a private interest, law enforcement is called in and investigations begin. The air hangs heavy with the odor of ethical impropriety and lawbreaking. Political opponents of the administration cheer on the investigations and call for more. The talk shows fill up with commentators, many of them opponents of the administration, who "analyze" the potential lawbreaking. Few of these investigations ever find much evidence of indictable criminal behavior, but that is not the point. They provide splendid opportunities to throw an incumbent administration off stride and that, not more integrity in government, is what most of the cheerleaders seek.

We need laws and policies that protect the integrity of government operations—but not the laws and policies that currently prevail. We need regulations that are based on careful analysis of what is broken and what can be done realistically to fix it. We need to start with the premise that we cannot set effective traps for every larcenous thought and every venal act. We cannot make government scandal proof. In fact, the costs of trying to make government scandal proof greatly outweigh the benefits.

It is especially important in formulating a rational ethics policy to identify those elements of the political system that are worthy of preserving and to protect them from damage caused by ill-conceived ethics regulation. Most important among the qualities to be protected are the in-and-outer system for staffing the senior levels of government, the democratic value of political accountability, and the essential need for political comity.

The presidential appointments process—the in-and-outer system—was one of the great inventions of American political genius. It sought to tie the government directly to the people by ensuring a constant flow of new people, drawn from real lives in the real world of affairs, into the government for tours of energetic and creative service. Americans early on rejected the notion that government was an enterprise best left to a governing class, turning instead to a new idea: that government should be the responsibility of the best of the governed.

And for much of U.S. history it was that, as men and women such as Josephus Daniels, Henry Stimson, Herbert Hoover, Frances Perkins, and John Foster Dulles set aside their private pursuits, often at great financial sacrifice, to lend their estimable talents to the service of their country.

In those times, Americans looked with pride on their appointments process and the kinds of leaders it produced. Transitions were swift and smooth. The White House called, the candidate accepted the job, he or she was at work in Washington a few weeks later. Investigations, questionnaires, hostile confirmations, bludgeoning of reputations all were largely unknown. Public service was an honor and, to most of those who undertook it, it felt that way.

But those are times past, and increasingly—and distressingly—these days the appointments process and the ethics policies are hostile and alien to the very Americans who should be welcomed to public service. There can be no higher goal in fixing the ethics policies than restoring the appeal of public service to the most talented American citizens.

Beyond that, we also need to free our elected presidents to lead the government. Imagine what it would be like to be the newly selected chief executive officer of a large corporation, to finally be in a job you had sought and prepared for all your adult life. The board of directors chose you as the best available candidate for the job and they gave you a clear assignment: "Increase the profitability of this company to the benefit of its shareholders. We will hold you accountable for that."

But as you prepared to start this new job, the chairman of the board pulled you aside and said, "Oh, by the way, did we mention that any of the people you choose to run the divisions of the company will have to be approved by a committee of your worst enemies, each of whom has a veto over your choices? And they will expect you to choose people who are willing to have every aspect of their private lives subjected to constant and penetrating scrutiny and to forgo any income that doesn't come from the company and to dispose of any financial asset that might benefit from the decisions they make for the company." What chief executive would tolerate those kinds of constraints on his or her ability to manage the company?

Yet that is very close to the situation encountered by modern American presidents. The voters will hold them accountable for their performance in office, but they have little freedom to choose whomever they feel they need to run the government efficiently and successfully. The current ethics policies do a great disservice to the value of political accountability, and that value needs to be restored.

Those ethics policies also contribute to the contemporary assault on political comity. American politics has always been vigorously contested, and public policies usually are the product of years of struggle. But the political combatants generally respected and trusted each other. They may have given the full measure of their intellects and energies to the day's political battles, but they could then have a drink together or play golf together or otherwise appreciate each other's company when the political work was done. The American political system has survived stiff challenges in no small part because this kind of comity helped political opponents to work together to seek consensual solutions to national problems.

But political comity has been dwindling in recent years. There are many reasons for this, and the decline cannot be attributed to any single cause. But no contemporary commentator could overlook the role that ethics policies have played in driving deep wedges of distrust between those who practice politics in Washington. It is one thing to remain a friend with a political adversary who opposes you in debate, even one whose party beats yours in an election. It is another to maintain an effective working relationship with an adversary who constantly charges you with ethical improprieties or crimes, who mounts or encourages investigations of your behavior, who threatens not just to defeat you politically but to put you in jail.

Washington politics has come to that. How does an appointee work closely with a Senate committee that delayed his confirmation for months while it investigated his personal business dealings? How does a cabinet secretary maintain positive relations with party leaders in Congress who call for an independent counsel to investigate her? How does a president build majority coalitions that require the participation of members of Congress whose committees spend more time investigating him than holding hearings on his policy proposals?

The contemporary record provides a ready answer. They do not. Washington politics—the necessary and mutually respectful interaction among opposing forces that is essential to the success of any democracy—is in grave disrepair. And to the substantial extent that the opportunities for abuse inherent in current ethics policy have contributed to this, they must be reconsidered and reconfigured.

Changing Directions

Can there be less ethics regulation without less ethics? We believe so. In fact, we believe that some ethics deregulation will improve the overall quality of the public service and of government performance with no discernible impact on public integrity. We can draw no other conclusion from our findings but that much of what now constitutes ethics policy is overkill or misses its target or imposes costs that greatly outweigh any real or potential benefits.

Deregulation will make public service more attractive to talented people. It will speed up the emplacement of new administrations. Politics will be de-fanged in important ways. Presidents will be freer to concentrate on their policy and administrative leadership responsibilities. The American people will have less reason for skepticism about government integrity.

Will there be more ethical misbehavior as a result of deregulation? Perhaps, but we doubt that the impact will be significant—if there is one at all. Most federal officials stay out of trouble; most did so before the ethics regulations were put in place. There is no reason to expect that to change in the future. In a work force of more than 2.7 million civilian federal employees, a few will always seek opportunities for self-enrichment. We do not believe our proposals for deregulation will encourage an increase in that small number or prevent the detection and punishment of those who cross the line. If there is some small risk of more misbehavior or less detection, we believe the benefits of deregulation more than justify that risk.

Set High and Clear Standards of Conduct

Nothing we propose here would do away with standards of conduct for federal employees. We believe those standards should be set high and should be clearly stated. For those behaviors that clearly constitute crimes—bribery, extortion, kickbacks, supplementations of salary, for example—criminal penalties should continue and be vigorously enforced. The important principle that public service is a public trust should not be compromised, and violations of that trust are intolerable.

Equally important, the federal government should maintain active programs of training and orientation for federal employees, especially those appointees who do not have a long background in public service. These programs should communicate the values of an honest public service and focus on the kinds of specific situations in which employees need to recognize the existence of ethical issues and to be well equipped to deal with them.

We admire the work that the Office of Government Ethics (OGE) and many of the agency ethics officers have done to develop and steadily improve such programs. Their contributions will continue to be the central element of federal initiatives in support of government integrity.

We also find much to admire in a statement of ethical principles for public servants issued in 1992 by the Council for Excellence in Government. These principles are listed in box 7–1.

Curtail Financial Disclosure Requirements

To many proponents of current ethics policy, public disclosure is the cornerstone. We disagree. We believe that much of ethics policy has become unfortunately ritualistic and that financial disclosure is the greatest empty ritual of them all.

We do not believe that the goal of government integrity would suffer any great loss if all financial disclosure requirements were eliminated. We find little persuasive evidence that financial disclosure alters the perceptions of public officials or enables better detection of misbehavior. We have found, however, that financial disclosure is a painful requirement deeply disliked by nearly all who endure it and sufficient in some cases to deter able people from entering public service. It is a burden on recruitment by presidents, and it contributes to the sluggish transition to new administrations. More than that, it nourishes some of Washington's worst political impulses by giving an administration's enemies fodder for attacks on its members—attacks that not only wrongly damage the reputations of appointees but also undermine valuable public support for the president.

We also note the irony that at a time in U.S. history when the federal government is deeply concerned about issues of personal privacy for its citizens, it imposes disclosure policies that invade the personal privacy of those who are willing to enter public service. We understand that public officials cannot always be judged by the same standards as private citizens and that some sacrifices are inevitable for those who enter public service. But we believe those should be necessary sacrifices only and that a heavy burden of proof should be placed on those who seek to impose them. Perhaps Dennis F. Thompson, Harvard professor and ethics specialist, put it most clearly when he said, "The private lives of public officials deserve protection because the privacy of all citizens has value."[6]

But there is another dimension to the privacy issue, expressed in the concern of Professor John A. Rohr, a specialist in the training of public servants:

> The problem with [public financial disclosure] is that we could end up with a public service dominated by people who are insensitive to the value of privacy. Because they had to sacrifice their privacy to the

Box 7-1. *Ethical Principles for Public Servants Issued by the Council for Excellence in Government*

Integrity requires of you the consistent pursuit of the merits. Your willingness to speak up, to argue, to question, and to criticize is as essential to determination of the merits as the readiness to invite ideas, encourage debate, and accept criticism.

Integrity also requires of you the courage to insist on what you believe to be right and the fortitude to refuse to go along with what you believe to be ethically wrong. You can never be sure what is right and what is wrong, however, until you have listened to the views of others, weighed the relevant interests and values, and taken the trouble to understand the facts.

All hard questions involve tough choices between competing claims. These choices involve loyalty to one's organization, respect for authority, recognition of the policy role of political appointees, regard for technical expertise and institutional memory, responsiveness to the public's right to know, and sensitivity to the need for confidentiality. How good a public servant you are depends on how well and how honorably you balance these claims.

Greed is a far less common corrupter of public servants than ego, envy, timidity, ambition, or a craving for publicity. To know how to manage and keep these in check demands character and discipline.

The true public servant:

—will not act out of spite, bias, or favoritism;

—will not tell the boss only what she or he wants to hear;

—respects the competence and views of others;

—does not succumb to peer or political pressure;

—contributes to a climate of mutual trust and respect;

—refuses to let official action be influenced by personal relationships, including those arising from past or prospective employment;

—has the courage of his or her convictions;

—is not seduced by flattery;

—unflinchingly accepts responsibility;

—does not try to shift blame to others;

—can distinguish between the need to support an unwelcome decision and the duty to blow the whistle;

—and never forgets that she or he is working for the people—all the people.

But general propositions, as Oliver Wendell Holmes, Jr., observed, do not decide concrete cases. To deal with the latter your only recourse is to consult your colleagues, listen to your conscience, and think hard. Some of us also pray.

Source: Council for Excellence in Government, *Ethical Principles for Public Servants* (1998).

public good, they might not be terribly squeamish about asking the
rest of us to do the same.

. . . A diminished concern for privacy would be particularly dan-
gerous in administrative personnel who often deal more directly with
the public than is customary in elected officials. The public interest
would not be well-served by a bureaucracy staffed by men and women
insensitive to the felt needs—indeed the passion—for privacy one
expects from the citizens of a liberal democracy. We do not want
bureaucrats inured to these feelings through systematic violations of
their own privacy. Financial disclosure must not encourage in government personnel the idea that privacy is of importance only to
those who have something to hide.[7]

In our opinion, no financial disclosure requirements of any kind should
be imposed on career government employees. Though hundreds of thousands of these employees now file annual financial disclosure reports, the
overwhelming majority of these contribute nothing to the quality of government integrity. These annual rites serve little purpose for the filer or for
the agencies into which they flood. Career government employees have
abundant training in the standards of conduct expected of them and in the
specific proscriptions on conflict of interest. If there is any value at all added
to that by financial disclosure, it is insufficient to justify the burden of this
responsibility or the invasion of personal privacy it inflicts.

We believe some instructional benefit may accrue when new entrants
into appointed positions complete financial disclosure forms as a basis for
consultation with ethics officials at OGE, the White House counsel's office,
or in their agencies. Especially for people who have never before served in
the federal government, it may be valuably precautionary to provide a listing of their financial assets and investments for conflict-of-interest analysis.
We believe, therefore, that financial disclosure should be required of presidential and other political appointees.

But we would limit that disclosure requirement in several ways. First, for
all but a handful of appointees, it would be confidential disclosure. Appointees would submit their disclosure report to a neutral agency, perhaps
the Office of Government Ethics, and the ethics official at their new agency.
These disclosure reports would not be available to the public. Senate committees could request them from the nominee if they wished, but committee members would also view the report in confidence.

Second, the financial disclosure forms would be greatly simplified. Appointees would be required to identify only the assets or sources of income that exceeded $10,000 in value in any of the previous three years. They would not be required to indicate the value of the asset or income source. They would have to identify only any asset or income source that exceeded the de minimis.

The current, highly detailed disclosure forms serve no one's purposes. Officials at OGE have often testified that for their conflict-of-interest analysis the actual value of an asset is of little importance. What matters is whether the value is more than minimal and whether the possession of the asset itself poses a potential conflict of interest. We believe a far simpler and more practical disclosure form can remove much of the burden of financial disclosure.

Proponents of current public disclosure requirements will be distressed at this shift to confidential disclosure for most political appointees. We do not share that concern. Our analysis of requests to examine these public disclosure forms made it clear that below the level of cabinet secretary such requests rarely occur. The vast majority of public disclosure forms on file at OGE are never viewed by anyone outside the agency. In light of that, and in view of the perceived loss of privacy by those who make these public disclosures, we believe there is almost nothing to lose and much to gain from altering the disclosure requirements for most appointees in the way we propose here.

We would retain the public disclosure requirements for the president, the vice president, and a small group of top presidential appointees. That group would include all appointees who head departments or independent agencies, the members of the regulatory commissions, and the senior White House staff with the title assistant to the president.

We believe public disclosure is appropriate for these few people because they hold positions of such importance and such accountability that the public can claim a reasonable right to know some of the details of their personal finances and the potential conflicts those might create. The people in these categories include nearly all of those whose public disclosure forms were most often requested for viewing between 1995 and 2000; indeed, they compose nearly the only appointees whose forms were requested.

But for the public filers as well we would simplify the disclosure requirement as we proposed for the confidential filers. It would only be necessary to indicate the possession of an asset or source of income that exceeded an established de minimis amount. We have suggested $10,000, a number we think realistic and appropriate. But reasoned political debate might fix the de minimis amount slightly lower or higher.

Nothing we have suggested here would significantly diminish any of the alleged benefits derived from current disclosure requirements. The most important and accountable officials in the government would still make public financial disclosure. Other appointees would make confidential instead of public disclosure, but little would be lost because almost no one outside the ethics firmament ever looks at their disclosure forms. Career employees would no longer be required to make annual financial disclosure, but we were unable to find any instances in which the existing requirements imposed on them contributed to a higher level of public integrity in anything other than theory.

Shrink the Use of FBI Investigations

The FBI investigations now required of all presidential appointees go way beyond their original intent in scope and purpose. What was instituted at a time of profound national concern over communist infiltration of government has become a tool for examining the character and reputation of leading citizens. It is a blunt and inappropriate instrument for that purpose. Most of the investigations take more than a month to complete, thus delaying the appointment of administration officials. They produce files full of uncorroborated rumor, gossip, innuendo, and known facts that are of little use to White House officials. And they are fraught with risk to the administration and the nominee when they fall into, or are leaked into, the wrong hands.

The same value of personal privacy that we applied in assessing financial disclosure requirements can be properly applied to FBI full-field investigations. FBI investigations should be required only when a compelling case can be made that their value outweighs the invasion of personal privacy and the delays that they impose.

In our view a rational investigation policy would look like this. No FBI background investigation would be conducted on most presidential appointees. Exceptions would be made for appointees to those positions with clear national security dimensions. The investigations that were conducted, however, would resemble the investigations now conducted on candidates for top security clearances. They would not delve into matters of reputation and character, of medical or marital history, or other such topics unless such inquiries were clearly essential to determine the candidate's fitness to deal with national security matters. Once a person had successfully undergone such an investigation, no future investigations would be conducted except for the limited purpose of updating the previous one.

The FBI investigation has taken on a life of its own in the appointments process. Presidential recruiters and counsels, who generally find little of value in the FBI files these investigations yield, are reluctant to call for their elimination because they do not want to appear that they are less ethical than their predecessors or that their nominees have anything to hide. So the FBI investigation requirement rolls merrily along, unchallenged and unchanged.

But it has costs, real costs, to the privacy of its subjects and to the efficiency of presidential transitions. The investigation produces nowhere near enough benefit for most appointments to justify those costs. While terrorists were plotting and implementing dreadful attacks on the United States in the summer of 2001, scores of FBI agents were protecting national security by investigating the backgrounds of eminent Americans who had been invited to join the new presidential administration.

What is wrong with this picture?

We believe that FBI agents should pursue real criminals and protect against real threats. Judgments about the character and fitness of potential presidential appointees should be made in the political process where they belong.

Reform Campaign Finance Practices

The real ethics sewer in the federal government is not the daily behavior of executive branch employees. It is the campaign finance practices that have evolved in the United States since the early 1970s. There is an awkward and ugly irony in this. In the same period in U.S. history when intense focus on the ethical behavior of federal employees has led to an elaborate regulatory framework, the unchecked growth of a fetid campaign finance system offers broad avenues of influence to the very interests the ethics regulations seek to keep at bay.

A senior federal employee must declare the full extent of her personal financial condition lest she make a decision that favors a company in which she has stock. But a member of Congress may accept—indeed, is encouraged to solicit—large campaign contributions from that same corporation even when its interests fall within the jurisdiction of a committee on which he serves. We call this a conflict of interest for the federal employee; we call it politics for the member of Congress.

The campaign finance system has invaded every aspect of American policymaking. Members of Congress and candidates for president receive hundreds of millions of dollars in contributions from special interests in each election cycle. It matters little whether they are in close races or even whether they have an opponent. The patterns of these contributions are clear. They go overwhelmingly to incumbents, and they are targeted by each special interest to the members whose committee and subcommittee assignments best position them to help the donor. That is to say that the influence-seeking and profit-seeking entities that make these contributions are acting rationally. They are using their campaign contributions to buy influence in federal policy decisions. Simple public-spiritedness is not part of the calculus.

But their influence does not stop there. A study by the Presidential Appointee Initiative found that of the first 320 appointees each of President Bill Clinton and George W. Bush, more than half had made reportable political contributions in the previous election cycle to the president who appointed them. Nearly 28 percent of them had made contributions totaling more than $5,000.[8] While no definitive evidence exists of any quid pro quo in these contributions, they repeat a pattern that has become increasingly common in recent decades: Campaign contributions are an important factor in determining who gets to serve in a presidential administration.

But there is a more important reason to reform the campaign finance process. It is a principal factor in declining public trust in the federal government. Most Americans do not follow politics and government closely enough to have a clearly sorted understanding of the complex mechanics of special interest influence. But even a highly disinterested citizen finds it hard to avoid stories about campaign contributions. They fill the air almost constantly and rise to hurricane force around election time. Powerful evidence suggests that distaste for campaign finance practices is a major source of citizen perceptions of government integrity. How, after all, can a citizen expect his government to make fair, unbiased policy decisions when he knows that powerful special interests are spending millions of dollars to help elect the very people who will make those decisions.

The American National Election Study asks respondents to respond to the following question: "Would you say the government is pretty much run by a few big interests looking out for themselves or that it is run for the benefit of all the people?" In the late 1960s, fewer than 40 percent of respondents chose "a few big interests looking out for themselves." In the 1990s, after several decades of spiraling and well-publicized special interest campaign contributions, more than three quarters of respondents chose that statement.

The public is clear and constant in its distaste for current campaign finance practices and its desire to change them, as the data in table 7-1 indicate.

No matter how many new ethics regulations we impose on federal employees, we cannot expect to restore citizen confidence in the integrity of government so long as we continue to permit the legal bribery widely practiced in the campaign finance system. The odor is so pungent and so widespread that no amount of regulatory perfume can disguise it. Americans will not find much integrity to admire in a government that puts itself up for sale every time it holds an election.

Beyond Policy

Over and over in the research for this book we came upon the phrase: "You can't legislate ethics." That is probably true. But we believe some aspects of any government's effort to ensure that its employees perform honestly and that its processes are protected from bias and inappropriate influences do require legislation. How else can the serious harm done to any government by bribery, embezzlement, self-dealing, or other genuine crimes be signified?

But we understand the point. Integrity is not just a matter of law-abiding because the law is too blunt an instrument to define or ensure proper behavior. Public employees act ethically when they adhere to high standards of conduct and when they possess sensitivities that cannot all be etched in law. In creating an ethical government, the hard part is accomplishing what the law cannot guarantee.

We believe the principal flaw in contemporary federal ethics policy is that it has too often sought to substitute formal regulations for the expectation of good conduct. As former White House counsel C. Boyden Gray has argued, "Ethics is, mind you, an elaborate legalistic ritual in which the application of multi-part tests substitutes for the internalization of values and the establishment of multi-level clearance processes replaces the development of supportive institutional culture. For government employees who must negotiate this ritual, the result is frustration and alienation. For citizens who hear all the ethics fanfare but nevertheless see government as usual, the result is disillusionment and cynicism."[9]

Table 7-1. *Public Attitudes toward Campaign Finance Reform, 2001*

"Do you support or oppose stricter laws controlling the way political campaigns can raise and spend money?"

	March 2001	April 2000
Support	74%	66%
Oppose	23	28
No opinion	3	7

"Do you think stricter campaign finance laws would reduce the influence of money in politics, or not?"

	March 2001	April 2000
Would reduce	66%	63%
Would not	31	33
No opinion	3	4

"Do you think politicians do special favors for people and groups who give them campaign contributions, or not?" If "yes," "Do you think that happens often or only sometimes?"

Yes—often	80%
Yes—sometimes	13
No	6
No opinion	1

Asked of those who think politicians do special favors for contributors: "Do you think this is a problem or not a problem?" If "yes," "Would you call it a big problem or not?"

A problem—big	67%
A problem—not big	20
Not a problem	11
No opinion	1

Asked of those who think politicians do special favors for contributors: "When politicians do special favors for contributors, do you think those favors tend to be ethical or unethical?"

Ethical	20%
Unethical	74
No opinion	6

Source: ABC News/*Washington Post* poll, conducted March 22–25, 2001. $N = 903$ adults nationwide. Margin of error ± 3 (www.pollingreport.com/politics.htm).

Many of those regulations were designed to prevent or trap every possible form of dishonesty or venality. They sought, through thousands of pages of densely worded regulatory language, to make government scandal proof.

But government can never be made scandal proof, certainly not through regulation alone. And aggressive efforts to accomplish that goal, even those lined with good intentions, have unintended consequences and side effects that are often as harmful as the scandals they seek to avert.

The national failing has not been in trying to raise the level of federal government integrity. That is an admirable goal. The failure has been in the means chosen to accomplish that and in the one-sided public debates that led to the establishment of those means. The passion for ethics blinded policymakers to the costs of ethics policies, especially the deterrents to those who might have entered public service and the heavy and uncomfortable burdens placed on those who did. "In an orgy of virtue," Professor Bayless Manning wrote in the midst of all this, "we seem to lose our grip on decency."[10]

A sound ethics policy requires a firm legislative base to establish the boundaries of legal activity, to create aspirational standards of conduct, and to create and fund a small number of ethics counselors, trainers, and enforcers. But no complete ethics policy can stand on legislation alone. At least two other ingredients are also essential.

One of those is accountability. We have argued throughout this book that contemporary ethics policy is an assault on the important democratic value of accountability. Too often ethics policies seem to be built on the wrongheaded notion of every man for himself. Only the ethics violator is responsible for the violation, and the responsibility is usually legal, not political. When ethics violations occur, the perpetrator should be punished, but no one else bears responsibility.

From that bad principle only bad policy could follow. And it has. Public integrity is the responsibility of everyone in government, but it is the special responsibility of those at the top. They should be held accountable for ensuring that their subordinates understand and adhere to high standards of official conduct. They should bear some of the burden of blame and corrective action when ethics violations occur. The common practice in American government of senior officials distancing themselves from the mistakes and corrupt acts of their subordinates is unacceptable. The senior official should be held accountable for the quality of government integrity wherever his or her jurisdiction extends.

But such accountability is often difficult to apply, and the best way to enforce it is through politics, not through the criminal justice system or through endless congressional and independent counsel investigations. When there is clear breach of law, a public employee should be prosecuted. An official who violates the public trust without breaking the law should resign. If he fails to do so independently, then he should be fired. In some circumstances as well, the superior in whose jurisdiction the violation occurred should also offer to resign or, failing that, should be held to account by the president. If high standards of conduct are to be the norm among public employees, the quick removal by resignation or termination of those who violate those standards must be expected.

The framers of the Constitution were not blind to the importance of accountability. They came to the conclusion that the president should be the appointing authority because that was essential to clarify who bore responsibility for the performance of executive branch employees. "The sole and undivided responsibility of one man will naturally beget a livelier sense of duty and a more exact regard to reputation," Alexander Hamilton wrote in the Federalist No. 76. "He will, on this account, feel himself under stronger obligations, and more interested to investigate with care the qualities requisite to the stations to be filled, and to prefer with impartiality the persons who may have the fairest pretensions to them." The senior officials of the executive branch serve "at the pleasure of the president." And that pleasure ought to vanish when standards of conduct are violated.

The framers established an important mechanism of accountability for presidents: elections. They trusted the public to keep its government honest by the simple device of denying incumbency to those whose administrations were not. But they also understood that these were not simple judgments and that the diversity of voter perceptions and opinions was as good a filter as any for making them. "In most cases," Professor Steven Calabresi has argued, "the public is quite capable of punishing wrongdoing by government officials without any need for lengthy supplementary ethics processes or for a special Ethics in Government Act."[11]

If it is clear, as we argue, that no amount of regulation can prevent all government scandals, at least not without intolerable costs and side effects, then it is essential that accountability mechanisms and accountability expectations are created to cope with ethical violations when they do occur. Presidents who want honest administrations must be prepared to set high standards and to fire those who fail to meet or enforce them. And citizens who want honest government must be prepared to exercise their vote as a swift sword of accountability when they fail to get it. No regulatory scheme can ever be a more effective guarantor of public integrity than that.

The other essential ingredient in a sound ethics policy is trust. In formulating the contemporary ethics policies, all sense of trust has been lost. Nearly all of those policies start with the assumption that no one can be trusted, that every public servant is a potential violator of the public trust

and should be examined and investigated and questioned relentlessly to fer-
ret out any particle of one's past that might yield a basis for disqualification
or future concern.

Many months are spent on this before even the most distinguished citizens have access to public office. You can bicycle across country, build a
boat, or have a baby in less time than it takes a new president to get his average appointee into office. Why? Because we now have ethics policies built on
such deep reservoirs of distrust that we must collect every possible assur-
ance of their honesty and constrain their potential for dishonesty in every
possible way before the president's nominees are allowed to assume public
responsibilities.

This is a counterproductive approach. It drives away able people who
have nothing to fear from such intense scrutiny, but who find it demeaning
and distasteful and do not want to be part of any government that thinks it
a proper rite of entry. It invites politically inspired employment of all the
available investigatory handles to undermine the president and his
appointees. It slows abominably the transition from one administration to
another.

The ethics policies, like much in public life, have contributed to the
establishment of an ethics culture that has become too deeply imbedded in
the collective psyche. It holds to the syllogism that because ethics is good,
any regulation enacted in the name of ethics is good. The defects of this
culture resemble those of the secrecy culture that Daniel Patrick Moynihan
described so well. "Secrecy," Moynihan wrote,

> is a form of regulation. . . . In the United States, secrecy is an institu-
> tion of the administrative state that developed during the great con-
> flicts of the twentieth century. It is distinctive primarily in that it is all
> but unexamined. There is a formidable literature on regulation of the
> public mode, virtually none on secrecy. . . . There has been so little
> inquiry that the actors involved seem hardly to know the set roles they
> play. Most important, they seem never to know the damage they can
> do. This is something more than inconveniencing to the citizen. At
> times, in the name of national security, secrecy has put that very secu-
> rity in harm's way.[12]

Similarly, in the name of ethics, much has been done to put good government and public trust in harm's way. When we surrender to an absorb-
ing but unexamined culture—whether secrecy or ethics—we too easily sur-

render our capacity for balanced judgment. The prevailing premises are overwhelming and unopposable. Common sense takes flight when the steamroller approaches.

The ethics culture is a culture rooted in distrust, in the notion that every public official and every candidate to be a public official is suspect. Whatever else they may have accomplished in their lives, whatever they may have contributed to their communities and their country, however well and favorably known they may be, we must assume the worst and undertake extensive investigations and throw up walls of fortification to keep their hands from the public till.

Can any of this be more valuable and productive than an alternative approach built on the fundamental assumption that presidents elected by the American people can be trusted to choose carefully in staffing their administrations and will aggressively enforce accountability on the performance of those appointees once they are in office? From where in all of American history do we draw the lesson that we accomplish more by expecting the worst of people than expecting the best? Yet that has been the premise of our ethics policies. It has not served Americans well.

A. Bartlett Giamatti, the late president of Yale University, once wrote that "if a society assumes its politicians are venal, stupid or self-serving, it will attract to its public life as an ongoing self-fulfilling prophecy the greedy, the knavish, and the dim."[13] That is the heavy risk Americans bear on the road we now travel.

Notes

Preface

1. See, for example, Dennis F. Thompson, *Ethics in Congress: From Individual to Institutional Corruption* (Brookings, 1995); Susan J. Tolchin and Martin Tolchin, *Congressional Ethics: Glass Houses and the Politics of Venom* (Boulder, Colo.: Westview Press, 2001); Steven Lubet and Judith Rosenbaum, *Financial Disclosure by Judges: Functional Analysis and Critique* (Washington: American Judicature Society, 1989); Thomas E. Baker, *Good Judge: Report of the Twentieth Century Fund Task Force on Federal Judicial Responsibility* (New York: Twentieth Century Fund, 1989); and Jeffrey M. Shaman, Steven Lubet, and James J. Alfini, *Judicial Conduct and Ethics* (Washington: LEXIS Publishing, 1995).

2. Judith M. Labiner, *A Vote of No Confidence: How Americans View Presidential Appointees* (Washington: Presidential Appointee Initiative, 2001), pp. 6–7.

Chapter One

1. William O. Douglas, *Go East, Young Man: The Early Years* (Random House, 1974), p. 264.

2. Alexander Hamilton, *The Federalist*, No. 76, April 1, 1788, in *The Debate on the Constitution, Part II* (New York: Library of America, 1993), pp. 392–93.

Chapter Two

1. Frank Anechiarico and James B. Jacobs, *The Pursuit of Absolute Integrity: How Corruption Control Makes Government Ineffective* (University of Chicago Press, 1998), p. xiv.

2. Suzanne Garment, *Scandal: The Crisis of Mistrust in American Politics* (Times Books, 1991), p. 6.

3. Robert Moranto, "Thinking the Unthinkable: A Case for Spoils in the Federal Bureaucracy," *Administration and Society*, vol. 29, no. 6 (January 1998), pp. 625–26.

4. James Sterling Young, *The Washington Community: 1800–1828* (Harcourt, Brace, and World, 1966), p. 31.

5. The prohibition survives in 18 U.S.C. 205.

6. *Report Number 2 of the Select Committee on Government Contracts,* U.S. House of Representatives, 37 Cong. 2 sess. (Government Printing Office, 1862), p. x.

7. Vernon Louis Parrington, *Main Currents in American Thought,* vol. 3 (Harcourt, Brace, 1930; reprinted 1958), p. 23.

8. Timothy Rives, "Grant, Babcock, and the Whiskey Ring," *Quarterly of the National Archives and Records Administration,* vol. 32, no. 3 (Fall 2000) (http://americanhistory. about.com/cs/scandals1/ [October 18, 2001]).

9. Rives, "Grant, Babcock, and the Whiskey Ring."

10. Garment, *Scandal,* p. 3.

11. Samuel Eliot Morison and Henry Steele Commager, *The Growth of the American Republic,* vol. 2 (New York: Oxford University Press, 1962), p. 71.

12. "George Washington Plunkitt on 'Honest Graft'" (www.mindspring.com/ ~historic-ny/plunkitt.htm [October 18, 2001]).

13. See Edward Winslow Martin, *Behind the Scenes in Washington: A Complete and Graphic Account of the Credit Mobilier Investigation* (Washington: Continental Publishing Company, 1873).

14. See Frederick Mosher, *Democracy and Public Service,* 2d ed. (New York: Oxford University Press, 1982), pp. 100–03.

15. 18 U.S.C. 209.

16. Quoted by Nathan Miller, *Stealing from America* (New York: Paragon House, 1992), p. 262.

17. See David H. Stratton, *Tempest Over Teapot Dome: The Story of Albert B. Fall* (University of Oklahoma Press, 1998); and M. E. Ravage, *The Story of Teapot Dome* (New York: Burt Franklin Reprints, 1924).

18. See U.S. War Production Board, *Policies and Procedures on Dollar-a-Year and Without-Compensation Employees of the War Production Board and Predecessor Agencies* (Washington, 1944), for the board's description of its efforts to protect the integrity of its activities.

19. See *Report of the Subcommittee on Ethical Standards in Government,* Subcommittee on Ethical Standards in Government of the U.S. Senate Committee on Labor and Public Welfare, 82 Cong. 1 sess. (Government Printing Office, 1951).

20. President Harry S. Truman, message to Congress, September 27, 1951.

Chapter Three

1. The three members were Judge Calvert Magruder of the First Circuit Court of Appeals, Dean Jefferson B. Fordham of the University of Pennsylvania Law School, and Professor Bayless Manning of the Yale Law School.

2. Bayless Manning, *Federal Conflict of Interest Law* (Harvard University Press, 1964), pp. 5–6.

3. President John F. Kennedy, "Ethical Conduct in Government," message to Congress, April 27, 1961.

4. Robert N. Roberts and Marion T. Doss Jr., *From Watergate to Whitewater: The Public Integrity War* (Westport, Conn.: Praeger, 1997), p. 49.

5. Kennedy, "Ethical Conduct in Government."

6. See H. Rept. 87-748, 87 Cong. 1 sess. (Government Printing Office, 1961), for a discussion of these initiatives.

7. John W. Macy Jr., *Public Service: The Human Side of Government* (Harper and Row, 1971), p. 253. Also, numerous discussions between the author and John W. Macy Jr. between 1974 and 1982.

8. Lyndon B. Johnson, "Message Accompanying Executive Order 11222," May 8, 1965.

9. Macy, *Public Service*, p. 254.

10. Macy, *Public Service*, p. 254.

11. The American National Election Studies surveys indicated that the percentage of respondents who believed the government in Washington could be trusted to do the right thing "all of the time" or "most of the time" declined from 77.7 percent in 1964 to 49.3 percent in 1970.

12. Richard M. Nixon, "The Checkers Speech," September 23, 1952.

13. Gary W. Cox and Samuel Kernell, "Introduction: Governing in a Divided Era," in Gary W. Cox and Samuel Kernell, eds., *The Politics of Divided Government* (Boulder, Colo.: Westview Press, 1991), p. 6.

14. E. Pendleton James, "Lifting Barriers to Government Service," *Business Week*, April 19, 1982, p. 19.

15. Administrative Conference of the United States, *Ethics in Government: Proceedings of a Working Conference* (Washington, March 1, 1988), pp. 26, 34.

16. "Carter Signs Government-Wide Ethics Bill," *1978 Congressional Quarterly Almanac* (Washington: Congressional Quarterly, 1979), p. 835.

17. "Ethics in Government Act of 1977: Message from the President of the United States Transmitting a Draft of Proposed Legislation to Preserve and Promote Ethical Standards throughout the Executive Branch and for Other Purposes," H. Doc. No. 95-139, 95 Cong. 1 sess. (Government Printing Office, May 3, 1977).

18. S. Rept. 95-170, 95 Cong. 1 sess. (Government Printing Office, May 16, 1977), pp. 1, 21.

19. *Congressional Record*, daily ed., September 20, 1978, p. 30423.

20. *Congressional Record*, September 20, 1978, p. 30425.

21. *Congressional Record*, September 20, 1978, p. 30430.

22. *Congressional Record*, daily ed., June 27, 1977, p. 20958.

23. *Congressional Record*, June 27, 1977, p. 20966.

24. "Ethics in Government Act of 1977: Message from the President," May 3, 1977, p. 62.

25. H. Rept. 95-642, 95 Cong. 1 sess. (Government Printing Office, September 28, 1977), p. 24.

26. S. Rept. 95-170, pp. 21–22.

27. "Ethics in Government Act of 1977: Message from the President," May 3, 1977.

28. S. Rept. 95-170, p. 31.

29. "Ethics in Government Act of 1977: Message from the President," May 3, 1977.

30. U.S. General Accounting Office, *Action Needed to Make the Executive Branch Financial Disclosure System Effective*, FPCD-77-23 (Government Printing Office, February 28, 1977).

31. S. Rept. 95-170, p. 30.

32. *Congressional Record*, daily ed., September 27, 1978, p. H10876.

33. *American Federation of Government Employees, Local 421, et al* v. *Schlesinger*, Civ. Action No. 77-1985, January 13, 1978, p. 3.

34. *Congressional Record*, September 20, 1978, p. 30429.

35. *Congressional Record*, September 20, 1978, p. 30415.

36. *Congressional Record*, September 20, 1978, p. 30429.

37. *Congressional Record*, September 20, 1978, p. 30415.

38. "Additional Views of Representatives Carlos J. Moorhead, Robert McCrory, and Thomas N. Kindness," H. Rept. 95-800, 95 Cong. 1 sess. (Government Printing Office, November 2, 1977), p. 104.

39. *Congressional Record*, September 27, 1978, p. H10879.

40. S. Rept. 95-170, p. 32.

41. *Congressional Record*, September 20, 1978, p. 30418.

42. *Congressional Record*, September 20, 1978, p. 30474.

43. *Congressional Record*, September 20, 1978, p. H10881.

44. *Congressional Record*, September 20, 1978, p. 30423.

45. Office of Government Ethics, *Proceedings of the Third Annual Conference, 1982* (Government Printing Office, 1983), p. 53.

46. Office of Government Ethics, *Proceedings of the Third Annual Conference*, p. 53.

47. Office of Government Ethics, *Proceedings of the Third Annual Conference*, p. 55.

48. Office of Government Ethics, *Proceedings of the Third Annual Conference*, p. 57.

49. Interviews and discussions with J. Jackson Walter, former director, Office of Government Ethics, Washington, D.C., in 1983, 1984, and 2000.

50. Interview with E. Pendleton James, assistant to the president for personnel, Washington, D.C., July 13, 1981.

51. Office of Government Ethics, *Proceedings of the Third Annual Conference*, p. 43.

52. Office of Government Ethics, *Proceedings of the Third Annual Conference*, p. 43.

53. E. Pendleton James, "Lifting Barriers to Government Service," *Business Week*, April 19, 1982, p. 19.

54. Office of Government Ethics, *Proceedings of the Third Annual Conference*, pp. 39–40.

55. Terrel H. Bell, *The Thirteenth Man: A Reagan Cabinet Memoir* (Free Press, 1988), p. 42.

56. "Ethics Law Weakened by Fears of Job Exodus," *1979 Congressional Quarterly Almanac* (Washington: Congressional Quarterly, 1980), p. 543.

57. P.L. 96-28.

58. Statement by Rep. Carlos J. Moorhead (R-Calif.) quoted in "Ethics Law Weakened by Fears of Job Exodus," *1979 Congressional Quarterly Almanac* (Washington: Congressional Quarterly, 1980), p. 544.

59. Title VI of P.L. 95-521.

60. "Revision of Special Prosecutor Law Cleared," *1982 Congressional Quarterly Almanac* (Washington: Congressional Quarterly, 1983), p. 388.

61. P.L. 98-150.

62. Independent counsel law, P.L. 100-191; Office of Government Ethics reauthorization, P.L. 100-598.

63. Second presidential debate between George H. W. Bush and Michael S. Dukakis, October 13, 1988 (www.debates.org/pages/trans88b.html [November 20, 2001]).

64. Second Bush-Dukakis presidential debate.

65. P.L. 101-194.

66. "Federal Workers Hit with Honoraria Ban," *1990 Congressional Quarterly Almanac* (Washington: Congressional Quarterly, 1991), p. 74.

67. On January 20, 1993, President Bill Clinton specified these and other ethics standards for presidential appointees in Executive Order 12834.

68. Quotes in this paragraph are from "Clinton Announces New Ethics Standards," *1992 Congressional Quarterly Almanac* (Washington: Congressional Quarterly, 1993), p. 62.

69. It is noteworthy that in his last few days in office, President Clinton issued another executive order (Executive Order 13184) ending the five-year post-employment restrictions. This freed his successor from the need to follow a similar practice.

70. This is also the conclusion of a distinguished academic panel chaired by Alexander Bickel and Ralph Winter of Yale Law School. See Ralph Winter Jr., ed., *Watergate and the Law: Political Campaigns and Presidential Power* (Washington, American Enterprise Institute, 1974).

71. Stanley L. Kutler, *The Wars of Watergate* (Alfred A. Knopf, 1990), p. 579.

72. Kutler, *The Wars of Watergate*, p. 610.

Chapter Four

1. "Interview with Amy Comstock," director, Office of Government Ethics, Business of Government Hour, Endowment for the Business of Government, August 22, 2001 (www.endowment.pwcglobal.com/radio/comstock_frt.asp#full).

2. 18 U.S.C. 208 (a).

3. 18 U.S.C. 201.

4. 18 U.S.C. 203 and 205.

5. 18 U.S.C. 209.

6. 18 U.S.C. 203 and 205.

7. 5 C.F.R. 2635.

8. For a fuller description of the gift rules, see U.S. Office of Government Ethics, *An Ethics Handbook for Executive Branch Employees* (Government Printing Office, January 1995), pp. 10ff.

9. 18 U.S.C. 209.

10. 5 C.F.R. 2635.

11. P.L. 101-194, Title VI.

12. 115 S.Ct. 1003 (1995).

13. For details of these, see U.S. Office of Government Ethics, *An Ethics Handbook for Executive Branch Employees,* pp. 29ff.

14. 5 C.F.R. 2635.

15. 5 C.F.R. 2635.

16. 18 U.S.C. 207 (a).

17. 18 U.S.C. 207 (d).

18. 18 U.S.C. 207 (b).

19. 18 U.S.C. 207 (c).

20. 18 U.S.C. 208; 5 C.F.R. 2635.601.

21. 5 C.F.R. 2635.101.

22. David Martin, former director, Office of Government Ethics, quoted in Ronald Brownstein, "Agency Ethics Officers Fear Meese Ruling Could Weaken Conflict Laws," *National Journal,* March 23, 1985, p. 639.

23. Quoted in Council for Excellence in Government and the Presidential Appointee Initiative, *A Survivor's Guide for Presidential Nominees* (Washington: Presidential Appointee Initiative, 2000), p. 82.

24. J. Jackson Walter, "The Ethics in Government Act, Conflict of Interest Laws, and Presidential Recruiting," *Public Administration Review* (November/December 1981), pp. 662–63.

25. Fred F. Fielding, "What to Do When the White House Calls," *Directors and Boards,* Spring 1983, p. 9.

26. 5 C.F.R. 2635.401.

27. 5 C.F.R. 2635.401.

28. 5 C.F.R. 2634.403.

29. 5 C.F.R. 2634.404.

30. U.S. Office of Government Ethics, *Fifth Biennial Report to Congress* (Government Printing Office, April 1998).

31. Executive Order 10450.

32. Interview with Thomas H. Kirk, unit chief, Special Inquiry Unit, Federal Bureau of Investigation, January 23, 1990.

33. Information provided by the FBI and reported in Council for Excellence in Government and Presidential Appointee Initiative, *A Survivor's Guide for Presidential Nominees,* p. 49.

34. Kirk interview.

35. Council for Excellence in Government and Presidential Appointee Initiative, *A Survivor's Guide for Presidential Nominees,* p. 48.

36. Data from an internal study conducted by the staff of the Senate Governmental Affairs Committee, May 2001.

37. Quoted in Tim Weiner, "Leaders in Senate Demand F.B.I. Files on CIA Nominee," *New York Times,* February 28, 1997, p. A1.

38. Alton Frye and William Webster, "Nominees and Their FBI Files," *Washington Post,* May 14, 1997, p. A21.

39. Quoted in Mary Anne Borrelli, Karen Hult, and Nancy Kassop, "The White House Counsel's Office," *Presidential Studies Quarterly,* vol. 31, no. 4 (December 2001), p. 576.

40. Borrelli, Hult, and Kassop, "The White House Counsel's Office," p. 578.

41. The Ethics in Government Act titled this position a "special prosecutor." In subsequent renewals of the authority, the title was changed to "independent counsel."

42. General Accounting Office, *DOJ's Public Integrity Section: Case Management Policies Followed, But Closing Some Matters Took Too Long*, GAO-01-122 (Government Printing Office, January 2001), p. 20.

43. General Accounting Office, *DOJ's Public Integrity Section*, p. 23.

44. Transcript of an American Enterprise Institute Conference, "Ethics: The Revolving Door," Washington, D.C., February 14, 2001 (www.aei.org/past_event/conf010214.htm).

45. Some of those who did review the impacts of ethics regulations are Frank Anechiarico and others, *The Pursuit of Absolute Integrity* (University of Chicago Press, 1998); Suzanne Garment, *Scandal: The Crisis of Mistrust in American Politics* (Times Books, 1991); and Arthur Maass, "U.S. Prosecution of State and Local Officials for Political Corruption," *Publius* (Summer 1987), pp. 195–227.

Chapter Five

1. E-mail from Richard W. Waterman, professor, University of Kentucky, February 14, 2002. The study in preparation is Richard W. Waterman and others, "From the Court of St. James to Burkina Faso? The Presidential Appointment Calculus."

2. Though debates on public disclosure are full of citations of "Dr. Johnson's dictum," we have never been able to find this statement in his writings or in Boswell's life of Johnson.

3. Larry J. Sabato, *Feeding Frenzy: How Attack Journalism Has Transformed American Politics* (Free Press, 1991), p. 138.

4. Benjamin Ginsberg and Martin Shefter, *Politics by Other Means: Politicians, Prosecutors, and the Press from Watergate to Whitewater*, 2d ed. (W. W. Norton, 1999), pp. 28–29.

5. Lexis-Nexis, "Expanded Academic Index", *New York Times Index, Reader's Guide to Periodical Literature*, and so on.

6. Sabato, *Feeding Frenzy*, p. 181.

7. See Elliott Currie, *Crime and Punishment in America* (New York: Metropolitan Books, 1998).

8. U.S. Department of Justice, Criminal Division, Public Integrity Section, "Report to Congress on the Activities and Operations of the Public Integrity Section," mimeograph (1989), p. 26.

9. Paul C. Light, *Monitoring Government: Inspectors General and the Search for Accountability* (Brookings, 1993), p. 162.

10. Frank A. Micciche, "Inspectors General Report Billions in Savings," *Government Executive*, July 14, 2000 (www.govexec.com/dailyfed/0700/071400f1.htm [January 11, 2002]).

11. Suzanne Garment, *Scandal: The Crisis of Mistrust in American Politics* (Times Books, 1991), p. 114.

12. National Association of Assistant United States Attorneys (www.naausa.org [January 11, 2002]).

13. From unpublished government personnel records, reported by the Transactional Records Access Clearinghouse, Syracuse University, 2000 (www.syr.edu/tracfbi/findings/natuional/staff190899L.html [January 11, 2002]).

14. Robert N. Roberts and Marion T. Doss Jr., *From Watergate to Whitewater: The Public Integrity War* (Westport, Conn.: Praeger Press, 1997), p. 93. See also James Q. Wilson, "The Changing FBI: The Road to Abscam," in James P. Pfiffner, ed., *Governance and American Politics* (Harcourt Brace, 1997), p. 206.

15. General Accounting Office, *Financial Audits of Expenditures by Independent Counsels*, GAO/AIMD-97-24R, GAO/AIMD-97-64, GAO/AIMD-97-164, GAO/98-100, GAO/AIMD-00-120, GAO/AIMD-99-292, GAO/AIMD-99-105, GAO/AIMD-98-285, GAO/AIMD-99-105, GAO/AIMD-99-292, GAO/AIMD-00-120, GAO/AIMD-00-310, GAO-01-505, GAO-01-1035 (Government Printing Office, various years).

16. Garment, *Scandal*, p. 138.

17. For an elaboration of this argument, see E. J. Dionne, *Why Americans Hate Politics* (Simon and Schuster, 1991).

18. Gallup Poll, March 19-21, 1999. $N = 1,018$ adults nationwide.

19. As of spring 2002, a significant uptick in measures of trust in government was evident following the terrorist attacks of September 11, 2001. The likely duration of that change is unknown, but the change is unrelated to the analysis offered here.

Chapter Six

1. This strikes us as a conservative estimate. Discussions with scores of presidential appointees over many years have nearly always indicated that the time required to complete SF-278 for new appointees usually exceeds three hours by many magnitudes.

2. This discussion of appointee burdens draws from Council for Excellence in Government and the Presidential Appointee Initiative, *A Survivor's Guide for Presidential Nominees* (Washington: Presidential Appointee Initiative, 2000), especially pages 31–37.

3. This is the number of questions in the questionnaire used in 2001. During the Clinton administration, there were forty-three questions.

4. Council for Excellence in Government and the Presidential Appointee Initiative, *A Survivor's Guide for Presidential Nominees*, p. 41.

5. Terry Sullivan, "Repetitiveness, Redundancy, and Reform: Rationalizing the Inquiry of Presidential Appointees," in G. Calvin Mackenzie, ed., *Innocent until Nominated: The Breakdown of the Presidential Appointments Process* (Brookings, 2001), p. 206.

6. Data from an internal study conducted by the staff of the Senate Governmental Affairs Committee, May 2001.

7. Some Senate committees have procedures that permit other senators to view the FBI file as well.

8. U.S. Senate, Committee on Government Operations, *Study on Federal Regulation: The Regulatory Appointments Process*, 95 Cong., 1 sess. (Government Printing Office, 1977), p. 141.

9. Quoted in Craig Gilbert, "Thompson Still Waiting to Get His Staff in Place: Slow Appointment Process Hampers Many Departments," *Milwaukee Journal Sentinel*, April 22, 2001 (www.jsonline.com/news/nat/apr01/cabinet23042201.asp).

10. Council for Excellence in Government and the Presidential Appointee Initiative, *A Survivor's Guide for Presidential Nominees*, p. 33.

11. See William B. Gould IV, *Labored Relations: Law, Politics, and the NLRB* (MIT Press, 2000), pp. 26–27.

12. Gould, *Labored Relations,* p. 41.

13. Robert M. Gates, "Taking the Heat," *New York Times,* March 19, 1997, p. A21.

14. Claudia Dreifus, "Jocelyn Elders," *New York Times Magazine,* January 30, 1994, p. 18.

15. Quoted in "Assault by Legislators Prompts Anthony Lake to Ask President Clinton to Withdraw Nomination" (www.reagnradio.com/HotTopics.main/HotMike/document-3.18.1997.6.html [December 11, 2000]).

16. Administrative Conference of the United States, "Ethics in Government: Proceedings of a Working Conference," transcript, Washington, March 1, 1988, p. 14.

17. National Academy of Public Administration, *Recruiting Presidential Appointees: A Conference of Former Presidential Personnel Assistants* (Washington, 1985), p. 26.

18. Quoted in Stuart Taylor Jr., "The Trial of a Top-Level Appointee," *New York Times,* June 16, 1983, p. A17.

19. E. Pendleton James, "Lifting Barriers to Government Service," *Business Week,* April 19, 1982, p. 19.

20. U.S. Office of Government Ethics, *Proceedings of the Third Annual Conference, 1982* (Government Printing Office, 1983), p. 57.

21. U.S. Office of Government Ethics, *Proceedings of the Third Annual Conference,* p. 58.

22. Quoted in Suzanne Garment, *Scandal: The Crisis of Mistrust in American Politics* (Times Books, 1991), p. 291.

23. Terrel H. Bell, *The Thirteenth Man: A Reagan Cabinet Memoir* (Free Press, 1988), pp. 41–42.

24. See U.S. Office of Government Ethics, *Proceedings of the First and Second Annual Conference, 1980–81* (Government Printing Office, 1982), pp. 9–10.

25. U.S. Office of Government Ethics, *Proceedings of the First and Second Annual Conference,* p. 11.

26. A detailed analysis of appointee compensation is provided by Gary Burtless, *How Much Is Enough? Setting Pay for Presidential Appointees* (Washington: Presidential Appointee Initiative, 2002).

27. Quoted in G. Calvin Mackenzie, "Appointing Mr. (or Ms.) Right," *Government Executive,* April 1990, p. 33.

28. National Academy of Sciences, Panel on Presidentially Appointed Scientists and Engineers, *Science and Technology Leadership in American Government: Ensuring the Best Presidential Appointments* (Washington: National Academy Press, 1992), pp. 2–4.

29. President's Blue Ribbon Commission on Defense Management, *A Formula for Action: A Report to the President on Defense Acquisition* (Government Printing Office, 1986), p. 27.

30. Larry J. Sabato, *Feeding Frenzy: How Attack Journalism Has Transformed American Politics* (Free Press, 1991), p. 211.

31. Data are from a survey conducted by Princeton Survey Research Associates for the Presidential Appointee Initiative. For an overview of the findings of the survey, see Paul C. Light and Virginia L. Thomas, "Posts of Honor: How America's Corporate and Civic

Leaders View Presidential Appointments" (www.appointee.brookings.org/events/january2001.htm).

32. Light and Thomas, "Posts of Honor: How America's Corporate and Civic Leaders View Presidential Appointments," p. 5.

33. Bayless Manning, "The Purity Potlatch: An Essay on Conflict of Interests, American Government, and Moral Escalation," *Federal Bar Journal*, vol. 24 (Summer 1964), p. 239.

34. Selected from "'Personal Data Statement' Questionnaire," a memo to all prospective presidential appointees from Alberto R. Gonzales, counsel to the president, 2001.

35. Steven G. Calabresi, "Some Structural Consequences of the Increased Use of Ethics Probes as Political Weapons," *Journal of Law and Politics*, vol. 11, no. 3 (1995), pp. 528–29.

36. Presidential Appointee Initiative, "Confirmation Countdown," January 20, 2002 (http://www.appointee.brookings.org [January 20, 2002]).

37. The first public confirmation hearing was held in 1916, and many years passed before that became the norm.

38. Burdett Loomis, "The Senate: An 'Obstacle Course' for Executive Appointments?" in G. Calvin Mackenzie, ed., *Innocent until Nominated: The Breakdown of the Presidential Appointments Process* (Brookings, 2001), p. 163.

39. Paul C. Light, *The President's Agenda: Domestic Policy Choice from Kennedy to Reagan* (Johns Hopkins University Press, 1991), pp. 41–42.

40. Tommy Thompson, secretary of health and human services, speech, National Press Club luncheon, April 17, 2001.

41. See *Leadership in Jeopardy: The Fraying of the Presidential Appointments System* (Washington: National Academy of Public Administration, 1985).

42. Based on personal interviews with a majority of the directors of presidential personnel from 1978 to 2001.

43. Congressional Research Service, CRS Report 96–271 (Government Printing Office, November 18, 1996); CRS Report 96–985 (Government Printing Office, December 3, 1996); and CRS Report 97–93 (Government Printing Office, January 9, 1997). All three reports were prepared by Rogelio Garcia, specialist in American national government, Government Division, Congressional Research Service. Data for boards and commissions include fourteen positions for which incumbents' terms had expired.

44. Burt Solomon, "Appointments: Plodding Pace," *National Journal*, March 31, 1997 (www.govexec.com/dailyfed/0397/033197b3.htm [April 2, 1997]).

45. Claude H. Marx, "U.S. Officials to Be Named Later," *Investor's Business Daily*, May 13, 1997, p. 1.

46. Cindy Skrzycki, "Dozens of Federal Jobs Are Vacant as Politics Bog Down Appointment Process," *Washington Post*, August 2, 1997, p. A1.

47. Bill McAllister, "Critical Jobs Still Unfilled by Clinton," *Washington Post*, August 29, 1997, p. A1.

48. Quotes are from G. Calvin Mackenzie, "Appointing Mr. (or Ms.) Right," *Government Executive*, April 1990, p. 35. See also G. Calvin Mackenzie, "Starting Over: The Presidential Appointment Process in 1997," Twentieth Century Fund White Paper, November 1997.

49. American Enterprise Institute, "Ethics: The Revolving Door," conference transcript, Washington, February 14, 2001 (www.aei.org/past_event/conf010214.htm [January 22, 2002]).

50. From notes found after Vincent Foster's suicide, quoted in James B. Stewart, *Bloodsport: The President and His Adversaries* (Simon and Schuster, 1996), p. 283.

51. Quoted in "Capitol Hill Blue," December 22, 1996 (http://tridentgroup.com/chblue/cabinetdec22.htm [January 10, 1997]).

52. Calabresi, "Some Structural Consequences of the Increased Use of Ethics Probes as Political Weapons," pp. 522–23, 525.

53. Edward C. Banfield, "Corruption as a Feature of Governmental Organization," *Journal of Law and Politics*, vol. 18 (1985), p. 599.

Chapter Seven

1. President's Commission on Federal Ethics Law Reform, *To Serve with Honor: Report of the President's Commission on Federal Ethics Law Reform* (Government Printing Office, March 1989).

2. Frank Anechiarico and James B. Jacobs, *The Pursuit of Absolute Integrity: How Corruption Control Makes Government Ineffective* (University of Chicago Press, 1998), p. 12.

3. This figure is calculated by multiplying the averages of 262,138 OGE-450 confidential disclosure forms and 21,019 SF-278 public disclosure forms filed each year between 1995 and 2000 by an average of 1.5 hours to complete the OGE-450 form and 3 hours to complete the SF-278 form. The data and the estimates are provided by the Office of Government Ethics.

4. Presidential Appointee Initiative, "Gaps on the Front Lines of the War against Terrorism," November 1, 2001 (www.appointee.brookings.org/news/gappositions_terrorism.htm [January 17, 2002]).

5. Richard E. Neustadt, *Presidential Power and the Modern Presidents* (Free Press, 1990), p. 74.

6. Dennis F. Thompson, *Political Ethics and Public Office* (Harvard University Press, 1987), p. 147.

7. John A. Rohr, "Financial Disclosure: Power in Search of Policy," *Public Personnel Management Journal*, vol. 10, no. 1 (1981), p. 32.

8. Presidential Appointee Initiative, "Campaign Contributions and Presidential Appointments," September 6, 2001 (www.appointee.brookings.org/events/contributionsappts.pdf [January 19, 2002]).

9. Transcript of an American Enterprise Institute conference, "Ethics: The Revolving Door," Washington, D.C., February 14, 2001 (www.aei.org/past_event/conf010214.htm).

10. Bayless Manning, "The Purity Potlatch: An Essay on Conflicts of Interest, American Government, and Moral Escalation," *Federal Bar Journal*, vol. 24 (1964), p. 254.

11. Steven G. Calabresi,. "Some Structural Consequences of the Increased Use of Ethics Probes as Political Weapons," *Journal of Law and Politics*, vol. 11, no. 3 (1995), p. 531.

12. Daniel Patrick Moynihan, *Secrecy* (Yale University Press, 1998), pp. 59–60.

13. A. Bartlett Giamatti, *The University and the Public Interest* (Atheneum, 1981), p. 168.

Index